# Coming up for Care

*Assessing the post-hospital needs of older patients*

**Judith Healy**
**Anna Thomas**
**John Seargeant**
**Christina Victor**

Policy Studies Institute

UNIVERSITY OF WESTMINSTER

*PSI is a wholly owned subsidiary of the University of Westminster*





A CIP catalogue record for this book is available from the British Library.

ISBN 0 85374 767 9
PSI Report No. 866

Typeset by PCS Mapping & DTP, Newcastle upon Tyne
Printed by Athenaeum Press, Gateshead, Tyne and Wear

For further information contact
Policy Studies Institute, 100 Park Village East, London NW1 3SR
Tel: 0171 468 0468  Fax: 0171 468 2201  Email: pubs@psi.org.uk

**Coming up for Care**

# Contents

## Part III Patients and Services

## Part IV Conclusions

# List of tables, figures and boxes

## Tables

## Figures



## Boxes

# Acknowledgements

The research upon which this book is based was supported by a grant from the Department of Health, Policy Research Programme, Human Resources and Effectiveness Initiative.

This work was undertaken by Policy Studies Institute, who received funding from the Department of Health; the views expressed in this publication are those of the authors and not necessarily those of the Department of Health.

The authors are grateful to the members of the Department of Health advisory group and also to the anonymous reviewers of the study report. We would also like to thank the following people.

Tracey Warren, Adrienne Muir, Dominic Moody and Joseph Traynor of Policy Studies Institute helped collect the data from the patient medical records. Penny Swann and Siân Putnam provided administrative assistance. We are also grateful to the health and social services staff who patiently answered our questions and completed the patient follow-up form.

# Acknowledgements

*Part I*

# The Study

# 1

# Introduction

## Background

Older people being discharged from hospital may need various types of assistance, including community health services (such as district nursing and day hospitals), social care services (such as home help, personal care, equipment, delivered meals and day centres), or residential or nursing home care. Assessing the post-hospital care needs of older people can be a complex process that involves different organisations and different occupational groups. Such multidisciplinary assessment generally is regarded as desirable for patients since it brings together professionals with different skills and knowledge, offers an holistic view of a person's needs, and reconciles different perspectives.

Care assessment has been described as a 'litmus test' of the ability of health and social services sectors to work together (Social Services Inspectorate 1995:1). It also tests the ability of different professional groups to work together, since multidisciplinary assessment is regarded as essential for patients with multiple needs (NHS Health Advisory Service 1997:2). Further, the policy aim of community care is that the needs of the person should determine post-hospital assistance (Department of Health, 1989a). In other words, care assessment should be needs-led, rather than service-led or professional-led.

In the wake of the 1990 National Health Service and Community Care Act, this study examined, first, how care assessment was staffed and conducted in hospital elderly care teams across England, and second, which factors predicted the post-hospital community care services received by older patients.

The research aims are summarised as follows:

- to identify which staff assess the post-hospital health and social care needs of older patients;
- to identify the processes involved in care assessment;
- to identify different multidisciplinary team models; and
- to identify which factors predict referrals and post-hospital services including predisposing factors (such as patient age), enabling factors (such as patient having a carer), needs (patient dependency and health status), or the team staffing model.

## The researchers

This study was commissioned by the Department of Health, Policy Research Programme, Human Resources and Effectiveness Initiative. The researchers were Judith Healy (Principal Research Fellow, Policy Studies Institute), Christina Victor (Reader, Department of Public Health Sciences, St George's Hospital Medical School), and John Seargeant and Anna Thomas (Research Fellows, Policy Studies Institute).

## Study stages

This study proceeded through several fieldwork stages:

- a telephone survey of social workers in 54 hospital elderly care units in order to obtain an overview of care assessment in hospitals across England;
- site visits and interviews with multidisciplinary staff in ten hospital elderly care teams in order to explore different team staffing models;

- a review of patient case notes in order to identify assessment and service patterns for patients (N = 456) discharged from three selected hospital elderly care units; and
- a follow-up of community services received by patients in the month after discharge from hospital.

## Format

This report is divided into four parts. Part I introduces the study, discusses the literature, and explains the methodology. Part II examines the staffing and procedures involved in care assessment in 54 hospital elderly care teams, and in more detail in ten hospitals. Part III analyses the factors which predict patient referrals for care assessments, and the receipt of post-hospital services, in a patient case review (N = 456) in three hospitals. Part IV discusses these findings in relation to care assessment procedures and service outcomes for patients and draws out the implications for policy and practice.

The term 'elderly care' is used in this report since this is the term most widely used in hospitals – the site of this study. Social services departments prefer the term 'older people', however, as does the UK gerontological literature. The terminology in this area, therefore, is problematic but the 'elderly care' label has the advantage of being best understood and grammatically convenient.

*2*

# Background to the Study

## Introduction

This chapter discusses policy issues that formed the framework for this research. These issues are examined under the following headings: the demographic imperative; the health–social care divide; and hospital discharge and care assessment.

## The demographic imperative

Older people aged 65 years and over represent 16 per cent of the UK population (Office for National Statistics 1998). Within this sub-group of the population there are approximately 1.1 million people aged 85 years and over. Future decades will see an increase in both the total numbers aged 65 and over, and in the numbers of the very old (the ageing of the older population). The group aged 85 and over is expected to grow most rapidly, with perhaps a three-fold increase by the year 2050.

Older people are important in health policy terms because they are a major consumer group for health services. In 1994/95 those aged 65 years and over represented nearly one-third (31.5 per cent) of all inpatient admissions in England, 24 per cent of day patient cases, and 53 per cent of all bed days (Department of Health 1996d). The percentage of older people admitted to hospital annually rises with age from 12 per cent of those aged 65–69 to 16 per cent of those aged 75 years and over (Thomas et al 1998). The average (mean) length of stay in hospital increases from 11.7 days for those aged 65–74 to 21.2 days for those aged 85 years and over, and the median stay doubles from four to eight days (Department of Health 1996d). Responding to the ageing of the population (assuming current levels of mortality and morbidity) implies that considerable demands will be placed upon hospital services in the future.

## Relationship between health and social services

The creation of the 'welfare state' in the immediate post-war period was characterised by a division of responsibilities: the National Health Service (NHS) was responsible for the sick (with services free at the point of delivery), and social services departments (SSDs) were responsible for social care (for which charges may be levied upon the user). This division of responsibilities between health care and social care almost immediately created 'a contested boundary' (Means & Smith 1998a) between these two sectors and is an issue that remains pertinent. The needs of older people, who often present a complex web of inter-related health and social care needs, rarely fit into a neat division of responsibilities such as 'the sick and the frail' initially envisaged by the architects of the welfare state. This was recognised very early in the development of the welfare state when an MP stated that 'older people fell into the "no mans land" between the NHS and local authority because they are not sick enough for hospital yet need more care and attention than can be given in their own homes' (Means & Smith, 1988a: 172). One issue in particular, the discharge of older people from hospital, has long exemplified the continuing tensions over the division of responsibility between health and social care.

The relationship between health and social care agencies and their respective areas of jurisdiction have been matters of continuing debate (Alter 1990; Tester 1996; Victor 1997). This is well illustrated by the concerns expressed about the discharge of older people from hospital and the problems arising from the inability of hospitals to discharge elderly people, often with chronic health problems, to a more 'appropriate' environment. For older people, admission as a hospital inpatient often represents only one phase of their 'medical career'. Once the initial acute phase (a stroke, for example) has been treated, many older patients require continuing services which can include rehabilitation, home nursing, social care or perhaps admission to a residential or a nursing home. From a bureaucratic perspective, this may involve several different components of the welfare state (acute hospital, social services, community trust and primary care). Hence effective hospital discharge has always required collaboration between different agencies. This objective has been enshrined in various policy documents (Department of Health 1994; 1997d). Indeed, concerns about the failures of co-operation between these different agencies have under-pinned several of the attempts to reform the NHS (Means & Smith 1998a; 1998b) and are clearly evident in the rhetoric characterising the successive changes during the 1990s.

A significant body of research has catalogued the persistent failure of health and social care services to work together to ensure the effective transfer of responsibility for older people from hospital to community care, and sometimes vice-versa (Taraborelli et al 1999). Studies have consistently documented the ill-prepared nature of many hospital discharges (Townsend et al 1988; Neill & Williams 1992). These include the sudden unexpected discharge in response to a 'need for a bed', the failure to arrange transport, the failure to provide adequate or (in many cases) any after-care, and the failure to ensure that such basic needs as food and warmth are provided at home.

The issue of older people who are pejoratively termed 'bed blockers' is another manifestation of the problems resulting from the failure of health and social care services to work effectively together. However, 'bed blocking' is not a new problem attributable to the 1991 reforms. Concerns about 'elderly chronic sick' 'blocking' acute hospital beds pre-dates the creation of the NHS (Means & Smith 1998a: 164). Hence the concern about delays in discharging older people is not new but rather has been an inherent feature of health services for over 50 years. In fact as early as

1948, the British Medical Association (BMA) commented that 'unless sufficient (residential homes) are provided for old people then hospital beds will inevitably become blocked and the whole service break down' (quoted in Means & Smith 1998a: 164). Hence, almost since the creation of the NHS there was concern that the hospital/community/social care interface would become a bottleneck impeding the discharge of hospital patients. Numerous studies have, with varied methodologies, documented the extent of 'inappropriate' bed use, described the nature of the population so defined, and enumerated the 'unmet' care needs of this population (Kid 1962; Murphy 1977; Coid & Crome 1986; Audit Commission 1992b). There is a broad research consensus that the roots of delayed discharge often lie in the admission process; that admission protocols need to identify those people with 'potentially' complex post-discharge care needs; and that comprehensive multidisciplinary assessment is the most effective way of expediting a 'good' discharge (Taraborelli 1999).

Responses to the twin issues of inappropriate acute bed use and delayed hospital discharge have been varied. Researchers and policy makers have advocated two solutions: the improvement of assessment and discharge planning in hospitals, and the development of community based services. Timely and appropriate assessment of patients has consistently been advocated as a means of improving discharge. Within the acute hospital, these developments have centred upon the identification of potential 'problems' by improved assessment and discharge planning that begins at admission. In addition, various 'early discharge' schemes have been advocated, including community-based post-discharge schemes. However, few of these types of intervention have been rigorously evaluated or any positive benefit identified. Such schemes were usually local responses to perceived local problems. Yet the problems illustrated by hospital discharge involve structural tensions between health and social care services, which must be addressed at a national level. National policy guidance has been issued, therefore, following the post-1990 community care changes, including the recommendations in the *Hospital Discharge Workbook* (Department of Health 1994).

## Hospital discharge and care assessment

The implementation of the community care legislation in April 1993 made local authority social services departments the 'lead agency' for the assessment (but not necessarily the provision) of social care, but did not specify the 'lead professional' who was to conduct the assessments. A key requirement is that social services must assess the needs of individuals for social care. Clearly the hospital is an important location within which to assess the needs of older people for care. A variety of different activities, however, are covered under the umbrella concept of assessment. These include assessing individual client needs, determining eligibility, prioritising those most 'in need' (targeting), and arranging appropriate services (needs-led assessment). Assessment may also involve rationing services, the substitution of services, diversion of users between services (ie from institutional to community care) and cost-shifting (determining whether the individual, NHS or social services will pay).

Assessment therefore involves not only a determination of a person's needs, but also a determination as to which services would best meet these needs, and, importantly, who will pay. The aftermath of the 1990 NHS and Community Care Act has seen a major shift in responsibility for the long term care of older people from the national to the local level: from the National Health Service and the Department of Social Security to local authorities. Also, local authorities were required to establish a quasi market in social care: purchase was separated from provision, services contracted out, the independent sector was expanded, and user charges increased (Means & Smith 1998b; Bennett 1996).

The variety of tasks covered by the concept of assessment provokes ongoing debate over who should undertake assessment and how it should be done. Within specialist medical services for older people, multidisciplinary assessment is considered to be the most appropriate approach, and one that is endorsed by government policy (Department of Health 1994; 1995b). Whilst there is agreement as to the desirability of multidisiplinary assessment (especially on discharge from hospital), there is less agreement on the type of assessment, the number of professionals, and the style of team required to undertake effective assessment.

There is clearly an imperative for health and social care professionals to work together to ensure that the assessment system works smoothly and that people receive the needed assistance. Staff working at the critical health–social care interface have been urged to ensure the provision of a 'seamless' service for their clients (Audit Commission 1992a). The assessment of individuals is a key principle of the current community care policy. Whilst the different groups agree upon the principle of assessment, there is no consensus as to what constitutes assessment, how it should be organised and which professional(s) should undertake it. Further, there is little research to indicate how the new system of assessment is working, and what is the most effective grouping of professionals to ensure the best outcome.

This study investigated the care assessment of older people in specialist elderly care wards in a sample of English hospitals. It maps out the different ways that assessment is undertaken, and examines service outcomes for a random sample of patients from three hospitals with different approaches to staffing care assessment.

3

# Methods

## Overview

Hospital elderly care teams were chosen in order to study care assessment for two reasons. First, medicine for the elderly hospital wards/units offer an opportunity to study multidisciplinary 'best practice' (NHS Health Advisory Service 1997: 2). The intention was to focus upon the hospital wards likely to practise multidisciplinary assessment and examine which ways of working appeared most successful. In other words, we wished to draw lessons from good practice, not bad practice. Second, these wards treat many dependent elderly patients who were likely to receive a formal care assessment, and so offered a large study population from which to select a sample of patient cases.

This study was designed to proceed in three stages. The first stage mapped care assessment procedures in 54 hospitals across England. In the second stage, ten different team models of staffing care assessment were selected and explored. In the third stage, three hospitals were selected for a review of 456 patient cases.

Endorsement of the study was obtained from the research committee of the Association of Directors of Social Services. Permission was also sought from directors of social services departments in the selected local authorities. For the patient case review, approval was obtained from local research ethics committees in each of the three health authorities, and approval was also obtained from hospital managers.

## Survey of elderly care teams

A sample of hospitals was identified from *The IHSM Health and Social Services Yearbook* (Institute of Health Services Management 1996), selecting large acute care hospitals with a Trust budget of over £45 million, and a listed elderly care service. Seventy hospitals were selected to give a geographic spread, with a minimum of six hospitals in each of the (then) eight England NHS health regions. Each hospital was matched with its counterpart social services department (recognising that the boundaries were not necessarily coterminous).

The social services member of the hospital elderly care team was chosen as the telephone survey respondent for three reasons. First, they were expected to have a good overview of assessment procedures. Second, social services departments were designated as the 'lead authority' for community care under the 1990 NHS and Community Care Act. Third, social services funds the bulk of post-hospital community and institutional care. Social services team managers in 70 hospitals (and the social services directors) were sent letters asking for their participation.

The hospitals who responded to the telephone survey covered a geographic spread of NHS regions (Table 3.1). Of the social services departments, 54 out of the 70 agreed to participate, a 77 per cent response rate. The sample covered 54 out of 118 (46 per

**Table 3.1** Telephone interviews and hospital visits by NHS region

| *Health Authority* | *Telephone interviews* *Number* | *Hospitals visited* *Number* |
|---|---|---|
| Anglia & Oxford | 6 | 2 |
| South Thames | 7 | 1 |
| South & West | 4 | 1 |
| North Thames | 6 | 1 |
| North West | 6 | 2 |
| Northern & Yorkshire | 12 | 2 |
| Trent | 3 | – |
| West Midlands | 10 | 1 |
| Total | 54 | 10 |

cent) of local authority social services departments across England. The sample also included various types of local authorities. It was selected prior to the round of local government reorganisation in April 1996 when unitary authorities began to replace county and district two tier structures (Clements 1997: 583–593). The sample included county councils, London boroughs, metropolitan councils and unitary councils similar to their proportional representation across England.

Telephone calls were made during July 1996 to the nominated staff member. A telephone survey was chosen rather than a postal survey in order to obtain depth opinions. Three interviewers used a questionnaire for the 30–40 minute telephone call, which contained both closed and open-ended questions. The interview was based upon a structured questionnaire and the interviewer also made notes that were later transcribed. The team characteristics and work practices explored in the 54 telephone interviews included the following topics:

- coordination – whether the assessment procedure was coordinated, how, and by which staff member;
- team identity – whether staff met regularly as a team;
- complexity – number and types of staff involved in care assessment;
- assessment pathways – whether there were designated decision points;
- formality – standard forms, a hospital discharge protocol, eligibility criteria;
- resources – access to post-hospital services.

## Hospital case studies

One research aim was to identify and explore different multidisciplinary team models. After analysing findings from the telephone survey, ten hospitals were selected that included a range of team models, held some external factors constant, and had a large patient turn-over. The main selection criteria for these ten hospitals were as follows:

- size – 40 plus beds in elderly care wards;
- single site – acute elderly care beds in one hospital;
- similar boundaries – only one social services team based in hospital;
- complexity – the team should include staff from several disciplines;
- lead staff – different staff responsible for coordinating care assessment;
- formality – variation in whether procedures were formally agreed and written.

These criteria produced sixteen hospital teams. Four hospitals were reluctant to agree to a case audit and two with similar modes of working to others were excluded. This left a sample of ten hospitals. One-day visits were made to the ten hospitals between October–December 1996. Interviews were arranged with the consultant geriatrician, nurse ward manager, occupational therapist, physiotherapist, hospital social services team leader, and ward social worker/care manager. Semi-structured interview guides were used to explore their views on how multidisciplinary teamwork was conducted. Documentation on care assessment was also obtained.

## Patient case review

The final research aim was to identify which factors predicted referrals for assessment and post-hospital services. Three hospital elderly care teams were selected, after analysis of the ten hospital team models, in order to examine the influence of different staffing models on patient service decisions. Other external factors were held as constant as possible.

### Three hospital elderly care teams

The three hospital teams were selected according to the following criteria:

- they illustrated different staffing and procedures;
- they covered similar types of elderly care wards;
- there were sufficient discharges to accumulate the required sample;
- the hospitals were in similar socio-economic areas;
- one social services department covered each hospital catchment area;
- there was access to adequate (according to staff) post-hospital resources;
- the staff believed that the team worked well;
- each hospital had good patient documentation and comparable data.

Five hospitals met these criteria. One hospital declined to participate as they were in the middle of staff changes; another was geographically too distant to make regular data collection trips feasible. In the three hospital teams that participated, different staff took the lead role in coordinating the care assessment process:

- Team A – the nurse;
- Team B – the occupational therapist;
- Team C – the social worker.

## Patient sample

The medical records of all patients discharged from the designated wards (over nine months from February to September 1997) were pulled by the hospital in several batches and examined by our researchers. Patient cases were picked up consecutively, aiming for about 150 cases from each hospital. (The exception was Team C where only 114 eligible cases were achieved over that time.) These patient medical records were selected according to the following criteria:

- the patient was aged 75 years and over;
- lived at home before admission to hospital;
- was discharged home with or without services;

- or, was discharged from hospital to a residential or a nursing home.

The characteristics of the patient, and information on referrals and arranged services, were obtained from the patient medical record. Much of the required data was recorded on three forms (although the format and content varied): a referral form, an admit and discharge form, and a joint care assessment summary. In addition, other notes in the record were checked. The patient medical records proved to have good documentation, as shown later by the small number of missing values in the results tables.

This study had intended to use assessment forms as the main source of patient information, but this proved problematic. Although a joint assessment form was completed by all health care staff (and physiotherapists and occupational therapists usually put copies of their full report in the patient medical record), these joint assessment forms did not include a section for social services staff. Further, the social services assessment report was not lodged in the patient medical record but was kept in their office case records. Clearly, this suggests a separation in work practices between health and social services staff.

## Post-hospital services follow-up

Health and social services were selected to follow-up whether the services arranged by the hospital for the patient actually were received in the month after discharge. Information on district nurse visits was obtained through health authorities, and information on home/personal care and other social services through social services departments. The follow-up time period was set at four weeks in order to focus upon 'post-hospital care'. Agencies were sent a data collection form to ascertain whether patients received the services arranged by hospital-based staff. The data were available from agency computer central records (except for Team A where SSD client records were held by local area teams). The list of names forwarded included cases where the patient medical record listed a service as arranged, plus any cases with incomplete data, so that we could be confident that all post-hospital services users (district nursing and social services home/ personal care) were identified.

## Patient sample size and analysis

A representative sample of at least 450 cases was estimated as sufficient to detect a difference of 15 per cent or more, with 80 per cent power and a 5 per cent significance level. The first phase of data analysis examined the distribution of variables of interest between patients of the three hospital teams. To examine the effect of hospital team on referral for assessment and on provision of service, crude odds ratios and 95 per cent confidence intervals were calculated. In order to control for differences in patient characteristics between the three hospital teams, the adjusted odds ratios were calculated using the Mantel–Haenszel method. This method calculates a simple weighted average which gives more 'weight' to strata with more data. By generating stratum-specific odds ratios, it is possible to identify interaction effects between, for example, 'team type' and 'aged 85 years plus'. However, since the stratum-specific odds were consistently similar, the results are presented as summary odds ratios.

The second phase applied a multivariate model using logistic regression analysis. This looked at the effect of the team type on referrals and services, controlling simultaneously for the effect of the main variables hypothesised as influencing the choice of patient care. Likelihood ratio tests were used to compare the fit of the different regression models. Significant change in the odds ratio, when adjusted for the effect of a variable, was considered to be evidence of confounding. Variables were retained in the model, or removed, using a forward selection procedure, on the basis of their effect on the odds ratio of team type and the likelihood ratio test.

The main independent variables for patient characteristics included predisposing factors (age and sex); enabling factors (whether a person lived alone, had a family carer); health factors (the number of days in hospital, the discharge diagnosis, and the number of medical conditions); and functional need factors (the degree of functional dependency such as mobility limitations and a dependency score). Dependent variables in relation to referrals for care assessment cover referrals to the various professional staff. Dependent variables in relation to services arranged include the type and number of community health services, the type and number of social care services, and institutional care in a residential or nursing home. The dependent variables in relation to services received, in the month after discharge from hospital, include whether the referral resulted in district nursing services being received, and whether social services were received. The main dependent outcome variables include whether the patient was readmitted to hospital in the month after discharge, whether the patient died, moved away, or whether there was an unplanned residential/nursing home admission.

## Summary

The first stage of the study mapped care assessment practices in 54 hospitals across England, through telephone interviews with the social worker in each elderly care team. In the second stage, ten different team models were selected and interviews were conducted with the geriatrician, nurse ward manager, social worker and occupational therapist. In the third stage, three hospitals were selected out of the ten and 456 patient cases were reviewed. The differences between patient characteristics (demographic factors, enabling factors, health factors and functional need factors) and services (referrals for assessment and receipt of services) for the three teams were analysed using multivariate analysis.

[illegible] services, the age and [illegible] care services, and acute and chronic [illegible] nursing home. The dependent variables in relation to services received in the month following discharge from hospital [illegible] evaluating the [illegible] being received, as was whether social services were received. The dependent [illegible] variables [illegible] was [illegible] after discharge, whether [illegible] had [illegible] whether [illegible] institutional care home [illegible]

## 7. Summary

The first stage of the study [illegible] recommended [illegible] [illegible] selection [illegible] and [illegible] health [illegible] [illegible] and [illegible] analyses.

# *Part II*

# Staff and Procedures

# 4

# Care Assessment Staff

## Introduction

The health and social services sectors are labour intensive and staff are both a major resource and a major cost. Staff salaries account for 70 per cent of the NHS budget (NHS Health Advisory Service 1997). The health sector is highly professionalised and employs a wide range of occupational groups. The NHS has a shifting skill mix (the balance between professional staff and support workers), wide variations in the deployment of staff on similar tasks, and considerable variations in productivity as measured by workloads (Steering Group Report 1996).

Human resources planning aims to ensure the right skill mix: a sufficient number of staff with the appropriate knowledge and skills needed to carry out a job effectively and efficiently. One way of doing this is to define a job in terms of the tasks to be undertaken, the knowledge and skills required, and the level of responsibility, while promoting flexibility without excessive duplication in task performance. Cost effectiveness calls for deploying staff who can do the job best at the lowest cost (Armstrong 1991).

Care assessment is a key activity in hospital elderly care units since public policies aim to ensure that vulnerable older people receive the care that they need upon discharge from hospital. *Caring for People* (Department of Health 1989a) and subsequent policy documents all stress the necessity for collaboration between the health and social services sectors in arranging post-hospital care. Chapter 2 outlined the long history of attempts to promote collaboration between health and social services, however, care assessment also requires collaboration between different professional groups. Multidisciplinary teamwork that draws upon different types of staff is a central principle of geriatric medicine (Brocklehurst et al 1992), and is also endorsed in a series of government guidelines (Department of Health 1994; 1995b). The benefits of multidisciplinary teamwork for service users, however, is under-researched (Øvretveit 1993).

Divisions between professional groups constitute as much a barrier to service integration as divisions between organisations (Hall 1986). Abbott (1988) argues that the history of professions is a history of the strategies adopted by occupational groups to establish exclusive jurisdictions over certain activities. Care assessment, as this report goes on to show, is an example of such a contested activity. Each professional group believes that they make a necessary and unique contribution to assessing older patients. This professionalisation perspective helps explain why multiple assessments by different professionals of a patient/client are common, since an assessment made by one profession is seldom accepted by another (Healy 1994). The different professional cultures also perpetuate the social versus medical model debate (Dalley 1991). For example, social services professionals believe that an holistic assessment is inherent in the social model and that health professionals are less committed than they are to multidisciplinary assessment (Caldock 1996: 30).

Social services departments are the 'lead agency' in relation to community care and have been set a statutory duty to assess individuals who need assistance with social care. The 1989 White Paper (Department of Health 1989a) set out the responsibility of social services departments to assess the needs of individuals for social care and to organise services specifically tailored to meet those needs (para 3.1.3). The *1990 NHS and Community Care Act*, Section 47, requires the local authority to make a formal assessment of the care needs of any person who appears to them to be in need of community care. The *Carers (Recognition and*

*Services) Act 1995*, which came into force from April 1996, also extends to carers the right to an assessment of their needs.

The legislation did not identify the staff regarded as having the necessary qualifications to undertake a care assessment. The qualifications of assessors were not prescribed but left to local authorities (Social Services Inspectorate 1991). Social services departments typically define as accredited assessors social workers, home care organisers, occupational therapists and nurses, but could appoint anyone they regard as having the necessary skills:

> *The skills required of care managers may be found in a number of professions and will vary according to the needs of services users and the model of care management that is adopted (Department of Health 1989a).*

Although the geriatrics literature calls for multidisciplinary assessment, it is not always clear what this actually means in terms of staffing. A specialist model of team organization divides tasks between people with different skills so that a patient is assessed by several team members. A generalist model employs staff who can perform several tasks and can carry out an holistic assessment on behalf of the team. A multiskill model encourages flexible working with different staff able to substitute for each other, which means that a patient could be assessed by any one of several staff.

What sort of procedures are involved in a care assessment? The legislation and official guidance documents leave how assessment is to be done to local authorities. For example, there is no definition as to whether 'needs' should be viewed in terms of the level of physical dependency of the person, or their age, or extent of social support. The professional literature generally opts for a broad or 'holistic' perspective of 'need'. Kane (1985) recommended that multidisciplinary geriatric assessment should cover the following dimensions: physical state, self care capacity, emotional status, cognitive ability, environmental resources, personal preferences, social resources, extent of burden on the support system, and the services already being received. Such an assessment is a major undertaking, but Kane does make the salutary comment that it is possible to oversell assessment: nobody is cured by diagnosis, nor are anyone's problems solved by assessment (1985: 48). The point here is that more public resources might be devoted to assessing a person than assisting a person.

The main purpose of assessment is also left broad in the legislation since it may serve the interests of individual patients/clients, professional groups, organisations, and government budgets. Various assessment purposes can be summarised as follows:

- assess individual client needs and arrange appropriate services ('needs-led' assessment);
- determine eligibility and prioritise the most needy people (targeting);
- arrange the minimum necessary number and amount of services (rationing);
- allocate low cost before high cost services (substitution);
- seek community rather than institutional care (diversion);
- determine whether the individual, social services or the NHS will pay (cost-shifting); and
- protect professional and organisational jurisdictions (demarcations).

How common is multidisciplinary assessment? Our findings on which staff in hospital elderly care teams conduct care assessment are from a survey (conducted in July 1996) of 54 elderly care teams, based on telephone interviews with the social services member. These views were supplemented by interviews with nurses, geriatricians, occupational therapists and physiotherapists in visits to ten selected hospitals.

## Elderly care medicine

This study was conducted in hospital elderly care (or geriatrics) units. Geriatrics is defined as 'the branch of medicine which concentrates upon the clinical, preventive, remedial and social aspects of health and disease in the elderly' (Victor 1994: 223). The management of older patients has changed over the last decade with a one-third decline in the number of geriatric beds and a one-third fall in the length of stay in hospital (Impallomeni & Starr 1995). Some elderly care beds have been integrated into general wards, and more health care of older people is being provided in the community (Harrison & Prentice 1998). About one-third of hospital admissions are people aged 65 years and over and a small (but unknown) proportion are treated by the geriatrics speciality (Department of Health 1996d).

Elderly care medicine in hospitals is organised in three main ways (NHS Health Advisory Service 1997: 71–76). Most elderly care units in our survey were a needs-related service: patients were admitted to elderly care beds (often via other wards) on the basis of age plus health conditions associated with ageing (42 out of 54 hospitals). These health conditions varied depending upon the specialities of the consultants. Second, in an age-defined service, geriatricians controlled designated beds or wards where patients were admitted according to old age (8 out of 54 hospitals). Third, an integrated service admitted patients to other departments and called in a geriatrician if necessary (4 out of 54 hospitals). Of the 54 hospital trusts in the survey, nearly 80 per cent controlled or had access to more than 50 elderly care beds each with 86 beds on average. The selection of hospitals in this survey, however, was weighted to larger rather than smaller NHS Trusts.

## Types of staff involved in care assessment

The multidisciplinary ethos of elderly care medicine suggested that the composition of elderly care teams would include varied numbers and types of staff who spanned a three-way professional divide between doctors, allied health professionals (nurses, occupational therapists, physiotherapists and speech therapists), and social workers. The organisational divide is between the health staff employed by the hospital Trust, and the social services staff employed by the local authority. Hospital social workers have been employed by local authority Social Services Departments (not the NHS) since the reorganisations of the early 1970s. This division between staff employers has a profound impact upon the workings of these hospital teams.

Social workers in the telephone survey were asked which staff were involved in two types of care assessment: first, patients being considered for a nursing home placement (where a SSD subsidy may be required); and second, patients being discharged home with substantial support from community services. 'Involvement' was left undefined since this may vary from a ten minute discussion with the consultant to a two-hour occupational therapy home visit.

Respondents were asked to indicate the extent of involvement in these two types of care assessment by each staff member on a four-point scale ranging from never involved = 0, to always involved = 3. The results showed that nine or ten staff were usually or always involved (a mean score of 2.0 to 3.0), while another ten or eleven from inside or outside the hospital were sometimes involved (Table 4.1). The assessment of patients in elderly care units, who are likely to need a package of community care services or an admission to a nursing home, therefore is very much a multidisciplinary undertaking. Clearly, such a comprehensive care assessment is a complex and potentially costly activity in terms of staff time.

The five types of staff who constituted the 'core' members of hospital elderly care teams were the hospital social worker, nurse, geriatrician, occupational therapist and physiotherapist (Table 4.2). These were the types of staff 'always' involved in the majority of hospitals. This constitutes a very definite measure of multidisciplinary assessment. In over 60 per cent of hospitals, these staff were 'always' involved with patients with multiple needs: those who required an institutional placement (and a SSD subsidy), or a package of health and social care services in order to return home. These staff are discussed in the following sections in order of their frequency of involvement.

## Social services staff

Statistics on the social services workforce in hospitals from 1993–1995 showed that the number had increased while the skill mix had shifted away from qualified social workers. The whole time equivalent (WTE) number defined as 'field social work staff'

**Table 4.1** Staff involved in care assessment

| *Type of staff* | *Nursing home cases mean score (N = 54 hospitals)* | *Community care cases mean score (N = 54 hospitals)* |
|---|---|---|
| Hospital social worker/ care manager | 3.0 | 3.0 |
| Named nurse | 2.8 | 2.8 |
| Geriatrician/consultant | 2.7 | 2.5 |
| Social Services team manager | 2.6 | 2.2 |
| Occupational therapist | 2.6 | 2.7 |
| Physiotherapist | 2.4 | 2.4 |
| Nursing home staff | 2.3 | – |
| Liaison nurse | 2.2 | 2.1 |
| Hospital discharge manager | 2.2 | 1.4 |
| Nurse ward manager | 2.1 | 2.1 |
| Junior doctor | 1.8 | 1.8 |
| SSD occupational therapist | 1.7 | 1.3 |
| SSD home care manager | 1.7 | 2.2 |
| District nurse | 1.5 | 1.8 |
| Speech therapist | 1.3 | 1.0 |
| Dietician | 1.2 | 1.1 |
| General practitioner | 1.1 | 1.2 |
| Psychogeriatrician | 1.1 | 1.1 |
| Other hospital consultants | 1.1 | 1.1 |
| Community psychiatric nurse | 1.1 | 1.1 |

* Involvement score (0 = never involved, 1 = sometimes, 2 = usually, 3 = always involved)

declined by 7 per cent from 1993 to 1995 to 2,388; 'hospital team leaders' declined by 14 per cent to 379; and 'hospital care managers' increased by 47 per cent to 1,589 (Department of Health 1996c: 105). Nearly two-thirds of social services staff in hospitals, therefore, were qualified social workers or team leaders, and over one-third (a growing number) came under the general category of 'care managers'.

**Table 4.2** Staff 'always' involved in complex care assessment

| *Type of staff* | *Nursing home cases per cent hospitals (N = 54 hospitals)* | *Community care per cent hospitals (N = 54 hospitals)* |
|---|---|---|
| Hospital social worker | 100 | 100 |
| Nurse | 85 | 82 |
| Geriatrician | 76 | 63 |
| Occupational therapist | 69 | 74 |
| Physiotherapist | 62 | 65 |

The social services teams in this survey all (except for Hospital 5) worked from a hospital base, not from a community-based SSD office. Most social workers were assigned responsibility for particular wards; only four worked across the whole hospital (Hospitals 3, 29, 53, 54). These latter staff said that this arrangement strengthened their allegiance to the social services department rather than the hospital, whereas other social worker respondents (and the hospital staff) believed that a ward attachment made for better teamwork.

Three social work respondents worked in hospitals in which two local authority SSD offices were located. Fortunately, this was a minority pattern, since it was said to make for ongoing confusion on the part of hospital staff, patients and also SSD staff. This situation sometimes arises since local authorities are responsible for purchasing or providing community and residential care for people living within their boundaries, but a large acute care hospital may have a catchment area that takes in more than one local authority. Various SSD inter-agency arrangements are made in relation to care assessments of hospital patients who live in other SSD areas.

All social services staff said that they were always involved in 'complex' assessments (a package of social services or entry to institutional care) since social services department resources may be required. In other words, 100 per cent of the social services respondents in each of the 54 hospitals said that they were always involved in complex care assessments (Table 4.2). It was clear from the telephone interviews that most social workers saw themselves as the lead worker in assessing the social care that a patient may need upon discharge. Several quoted the section in the 1990 NHS and Community Care Act requiring that people needing social care must be assessed by the local authority social services department. Some other staff interviewed in the ten hospitals saw the role of social workers somewhat differently, seeing social workers as discharge planners and as responsible for implementing the team decision. This was certainly the case in one of the ten hospitals visited (Hospital 1, below). Other studies also have found that hospital staff see the primary task of social workers as discharge planning, which was given statutory force under the 1990 NHS and Community Care Act (Davies 1995; Rachman 1995).

Further, if patients need post-hospital social care, discharge planning might also involve the provision or purchase of assistance by the social services department. Hospital social services teams have since 1993 taken over the new task of purchasing post-hospital social services – either as in-house SSD services or from the independent sector (Lewis et al 1996).

## Hospital 1

This modern teaching hospital, with an emphasis upon 'high tech' innovative medicine, had several elderly care wards in the main hospital plus beds at other sites. Shortages of post-hospital health and social care services, and pressure to discharge patients, were causing tension between staff in the elderly care team. This was a 'consultant led' multidisciplinary elderly care team. It was unusual in that procedures were informal and forms not standardised. Activities were coordinated at the ward meeting attended by all staff and chaired by the geriatrician.

The team was led by a qualified social worker. The social services care managers (with no social work or other professional qualifications) performed all the tasks associated with care assessment including purchasing. These social services staff had low status, did not regard themselves as full members of the elderly care team, and were seen as facilitators of team decisions.

The telephone survey reflected a professional as well as an organisational view since 94 per cent of the social services respondents had a formal social work qualification. These social services staff mainly are referred to in this report as social workers, although there were considerable terminological differences. This study counted 18 different job titles for hospital social services practitioners. The variety of job titles was confusing, since people with apparently similar titles might have different qualifications and did not necessarily do the same job. Social services teams contain several types of staff with the main tasks split between simple and complex assessments, and between assessment and purchasing. Over half (54 per cent) the social services respondents also had management responsibilities, usually as team leader.

*Social worker/care manager:* The staff who undertake care assessment generally were titled 'care manager' in the wake of the 1990 NHS and Community Care Act. The number of people with qualifications other than social work has grown (as cited earlier), which is contentious since some social workers argued that all care assessments should be done by a social worker. For example, one team leader (who was social work qualified) said that there was a greater skill mix now in the social services team but that lesser qualified people are less able to handle difficult cases and can't predict future problems so that cases often 'blow up'. She did not accept the view that 'assessment is easy when you have a form' (Hospital 1).

*Home care organiser:* These supervisors of in-house SSD home care services have increasingly been re-deployed to care assessment. Many positions have been superseded now that more home care is contracted out by social services departments to voluntary and private agencies. Ex-home care organisers now undertake simple (or all) care assessments in some hospitals, do patient financial assessments, cost the services, send off the paperwork for authorisation, and order services once authorised.

*Social services assistant:* The care assistant (also called care manager, care coordinator, social work assistant, community care officer) carried out simple assessments and might also cost and arrange the purchase of authorised services. There was no consensus across the 54 hospital social services teams on the title, the qualifications thought desirable, or the scope of the job.

*Other positions:* Other administrative positions included a purchasing manager who did the paper work in contracting out for services. A placement officer might organise residential and nursing home placements. Social services clerical staff did a variety of tasks such as logging referrals and sometimes even determining eligibility. In the ten hospitals visited, the social services team manager said that more clerical staff were needed to handle the greatly increased paperwork since the 1993 implementation of the community care policy and the associated quasi market arrangements.

## Nurses

Nurses comprise over half of direct care practitioners in the health care workforce. The growth in the nursing workforce slowed between 1984 to 1994, but, contrary to expectations, the number of qualified nurses increased more than unqualified nurses (Steering Group 1996: 50- 56). The ratio between registered nurses and auxiliary nurses and aides in hospitals (the nursing skill mix) is a matter of continuing debate. The number of registered nurses in hospitals increased by 29 per cent from 1984 to 1994, rising to 144,147 in whole time equivalents (Department of Health 1996c:92). The trend in OECD countries over the last few decades is for qualified nurses to undertake four main tasks in hospitals (Stallknecht 1992; Alazewski 1995). The technical tasks of nursing have expanded (delegated from medicine), management tasks have expanded (delegated from medicine and hospital administration), care for the daily needs of patients has diminished (delegated to enrolled nurses and aides), while emotional support for and counselling for patients has increased (taken over from social work).

This study found that the 'named nurse' was most often involved, after the social worker, in complex care assessments. Social workers gave nurses an involvement score of 2.8 out of a

## Hospital 17

The hospital is on the outskirts of a large northern city. The elderly care unit had over 100 beds in acute and rehabilitation wards. There was pressure upon beds and shortages of community and institutional services. The assessment process was nurse-led with an emphasis upon high patient throughput. There were few multidisciplinary staff meetings. The high turnover of patients reinforced role and task differentiation.

Nurses referred, assessed needs, coordinated, requested both health and social care post-hospital services, stopped existing services when a patient was admitted, restarted on discharge, and requested simple services from the area SSD office. Multidisciplinary communication was linked by the nursing staff. Medical and nursing staff met on ward rounds; the other staff met at occasional case conferences convened to discuss complex cases. Consultants rarely attended such meetings and their opinions were communicated by the named nurse.

Social services assistants assessed and organised simple care packages and social workers assessed complex cases. Assessment was split from purchase. There was no devolved hospital social services budget and the area SSD office authorised services.

maximum of 3.0 (Table 4.1). These 54 hospitals (or at least the elderly care wards) virtually all assigned a 'named' or 'primary' nurse to each patient. Shift changes, high staff turnover, and use of temporary or 'bank' nurses meant that the named nurse often was not available, however, when patients were discussed in ward meetings. This made the nurse ward manager also a key staff member in care assessment (Table 4.1) through activities such as attending ward meetings, supervising procedures, and in some hospitals chairing care planning meetings. The nurse was the key staff member who coordinated the assessment for and the arrangement of post-hospital social and health care services in some hospitals. (See box above, Hospital 17).

Nurses have long undertaken many of the tasks associated with referral, assessment and discharge arrangements. Interviews with the 54 social workers, as well as interviews with other staff in the ten hospitals, identified the following range of care assessment tasks that were undertaken by nurses, although these varied considerably between hospitals:

- screen and refer patients after admission to the ward;
- an initial assessment for both health and social care post-hospital services;
- stop and start services from the area SSD office for current clients;
- request 'simple' services from the area SSD office;
- assess and request community health services;
- assess the extent of a patient's functional independence;
- contribute an opinion to health and social care assessment;
- coordinate health care assessment;
- coordinate social care assessment;
- make discharge arrangements.

As well as their traditional nursing tasks, nurses have been appointed to care assessment and discharge positions, as summarised below. Some positions predated the 1993 community care changes but others suggest a greater formal role for nurses in arranging post-hospital care for older patients.

*Care assessor:* Nurses can be accredited assessors under social services department regulations. Some hospital social services teams had recently appointed nurses as care managers with their salary paid by the Trust (for example, Hospitals 1, 17, 33, 46). Some of these nurses undertook only the health aspects of care assessment, while others (more controversially) also assessed social needs. One social worker commented that health visitors (qualified nurses with a community nursing background) had a better appreciation of what services a patient would need to return home and had a more 'holistic' view of an older patient than a ward nurse (Hospital 49).

Hospitals differed on whether ward nurses (although not formally accredited SSD assessors) could request services directly from local authority social services such as short-term delivered meals. Some social services departments in practice accepted a nurse assessment of a short-term need for post-hospital services,

## Hospital 33

The large teaching hospital located in a southern city had an elderly care unit of several wards in one hospital wing. Nursing staff coordinated the assessment process. The named nurse screened, referred patients, and coordinated assessment and discharge. A weekly ward meeting attended by all staff was chaired by the consultant and all cases were discussed. Case conferences were held for difficult cases. The multidisciplinary assessment form did not include a section for social services, and there was considerable duplication in information gathering.

'Simple' cases were referred directly by the nurse to the area SSD office, and 'complex' cases to the hospital social worker. A nurse home liaison officer employed by the Trust did nursing home assessments. A community nurse liaison handled referrals to district nursing. Occupational therapy assessed people who needed care at home and usually did a home visit.

and many accepted a request for services to be 're-started' for clients after their stay in hospital. The assessment of these 'simple' social care cases was a matter of some territorial dispute between nursing and social work. The nursing argument is that they are quite competent to assess the need for 'simple' post-hospital social care, and that this would expedite discharge arrangements. This issue is discussed further in Chapter 5. Hospital 33 is an example where the hospital nurse directly referred people to the area SSD office for short-term simple post-hospital assistance. In practice, the SSD office usually accepted this as an assessment and provided the service (see above).

*Discharge coordinator:* Some Trusts employed a hospital discharge coordinator, usually with nursing qualifications, in order to expedite discharge (for example Hospitals 17, 43, 38, 46, 47). Other specialist nurse consultants appointed by the Trust negotiated respective NHS and SSD responsibilities and arranged NHS continuing health care (for example Hospitals 3, 16, 27). These discharge coordinators concentrated upon cases where patients remained in hospital after they were medically fit for discharge. Some hospitals employed nursing home liaison staff, usually with nursing qualifications, to assess patients for nursing home placements (for example, Hospitals 8, 33). These positions had been established between 1983 and 1993 when patients were transferred from hospitals to nursing homes with Social Security subsidies.

*Community nurse liaison:* Many hospitals had 'liaison nurses' who assessed and referred people to residential placements, district nursing, and to practice nurses at GP surgeries. They were employed by a community health Trust, a hospital Trust, or a health authority. Such liaison between hospital and community improves communications and minimises discharge delays (Social Services Inspectorate 1995). Since the increasing workload of district nurses meant that they had little time to visit a hospital for consultation on particular cases, these liaison nurses were an important link between the hospital and the primary health care team, and between the hospital and nursing homes.

## Geriatricians

Geriatric medicine has raised its status as a medical speciality over the last decade or so (Brocklehurst et al 1992; Victor 1994: 224). Hospital geriatricians are a small but growing speciality whose numbers increased by 16 per cent from 1984 to 1994, rising to 1,986 in whole time equivalents (Department of Health 1996c: 85). Doctors are responsible for patient management in hospitals, enjoy the highest occupational group status among health care professionals, and are regarded as the leader of the multidisciplinary team.

Social services respondents said that the consultant always assessed nursing home cases in 76 per cent of hospitals, and complex community care cases in 63 per cent of hospitals (Table 4.2). The geriatricians (although some may have been general physicians with responsibility for the elderly) therefore were less involved in community care than nursing home assessments.

The view of the geriatricians interviewed in the ten hospitals generally was that the geriatrician initiates assessment, occupational therapists and physiotherapists assess, social workers facilitate by arranging services, and the geriatrician decides the appropriate services taking into account the various staff views. They attributed good teamwork to close communication facilitated by ward-attached multidisciplinary staff, attendance at ward meetings and preferably on ward rounds, and offices in close proximity to the wards. Most geriatricians thought that care assessment procedures had improved under the new procedures, with clearer lines of responsibility between health and social services.

Other staff thought that care assessment remained 'consultant led': 'basically what the consultant says goes'. Some social services staff, however, thought there had been a shift of power away from the consultant to the multidisciplinary team, which they attributed to social services purchasing power. One social worker said that before 1993, consultants were quick to recommend a nursing home and the family then applied for income support from Social Security. 'But now the consultant has to listen to our view if the patient is going to be funded by the SSD' (Hospital 9).

## Occupational therapists

The number of occupational therapists working in hospitals has increased by 76 per cent from 1984 to 1994, rising to 6,413 in whole time equivalents (Department of Health 1996c: 95). This is a large rise in numbers from a small base but there are still shortages (NHS Health Advisory Service 1997). Occupational therapists are also employed in the community by health care organisations and many are employed by social services departments.

Occupational therapists were 'always involved' in 74 per cent of hospitals in complex care cases (third in order after social workers and nurses) but less so in nursing home cases (Table 4.2). Occupational therapists in the ten hospitals visited worked to their own line manager and were assigned to elderly care wards. The occupational therapy departments also employed assistants to do routine work and handle equipment loans. One hospital (Hospital 27) was considering employing assistants who could work for both occupational therapy and physiotherapy departments. Occupational therapists saw themselves as occupying the middle ground between health and social services staff. They explained their functions as assessing the physical ability of people to

## Hospital 60

The hospital, located on the outskirts of a northern city, had an elderly care unit of three wards housed in a separate building. There were adequate institutional and community services including a jointly funded (NHS and SSD) post-hospital scheme. Occupational therapists played a key role in care assessment.

The named nurse screened and referred using a patient scoring system. Cases were discussed at weekly ward meetings attended by all staff, and case conferences were held for patients at 'high risk'. Occupational therapists ordered equipment from the area SSD, requested simple services from the SSD, and referred directly to the post-hospital care scheme. Hospital social workers concentrated upon cases where there were discharge problems, while assessment for long-term care was done by area SSD staff. The post-hospital scheme had reduced the need for comprehensive hospital-based assessment since services were 'fine tuned' after the patient went home.

manage in their home environment, organising changes to help them do so, and assessing patients for rehabilitation treatment. The nature of their work had changed, with an increasing volume of cases. They no longer did hospital treatment or leisure work but concentrated upon risk assessment and safe discharge. This often involved a home visit, sometimes accompanied by the patient, or a joint visit with other staff such as the SSD area home care organiser.

Occupational therapists believed that they did a thorough holistic assessment using standardised measures to assess psychological, social and physical functioning, supplemented by observing a person's ability to perform daily tasks. They thought that they had the competence to assess a range of needs, not just the need for aids and equipment. Social workers opposed occupational therapists 'naming services' to patients, however, since this raised expectations that were not always met. Overlap and tension between occupational therapists and social workers on care assessment have been reported in other studies (see, for example, Clark et al 1996). In some hospitals, occupational therapists were key coordinators of discharge planning for post-hospital health and social care in the community (see Hospital 60, above).

## Physiotherapists

The number of physiotherapists working in hospitals has increased by 29 per cent from 1984 to 1994, rising to 10,571 in whole time equivalents (Department of Health 1996c: 95). This is a larger occupational group than occupational therapy but there are still staff shortages (NHS Health Advisory Service 1997).

Physiotherapists were 'always' involved in over 60 per cent of hospitals in both community care and nursing home assessments (Table 4.2). This reflects the rehabilitation goal of elderly care medicine. The ten hospitals visited had a physiotherapy department and assigned staff to particular wards. Physiotherapists usually attended the ward meetings where patients were discussed. The physiotherapists concentrated upon mobility treatment, which sometimes overlapped with nursing and occupational therapy.

## General practitioners

Social services staff in these 54 hospitals scored general practitioners near the bottom of the staff involvement list in care assessment (Table 4.1). Many commented that they had given up trying to telephone GPs, who were too busy, and certainly not available to attend case conferences. GPs were usually informed about 'medical care' decisions, however, since ward discharge arrangements in these elderly care units included sending a summary to the patient's GP.

The *Hospital Discharge Workbook* (Department of Health 1994) urged that general practitioners be invited to contribute to post-hospital care decisions for older patients. Clearly, this has not proved easy in practice. Nor is it common practice in the community, according to other studies. For example, only five out of 62 community-based social services staff said that it was common practice to consult GPs when organising services for older people (Allen et al 1992: 251). The absence of GPs from care assessment for older people illustrates the difficulty of strengthening links between primary and secondary health care and between health and social care. The White Paper *The New NHS* (Department of

Health 1997b) announced the formation of large 'primary care groups' based around GPs with a unified budget to purchase primary and secondary health care. These groups are now functioning and clearly will need to establish better links with hospitals if older people are to receive 'seamless' care.

### Other staff

Staff from the area SSD office were sometimes involved before people went home with community services (Table 4.1). Where a patient was already a SSD client, their community-based care manager contributed to the pre-discharge care assessment via the hospital social worker or the ward nurse. The SSD home care manager or SSD occupational therapist might also undertake a home visit in order to assess the home as well as the client. A social care assessment thus often involved both hospital and community-based SSD staff. Where the hospital social services team did not control a budget for post-hospital care, the area SSD team was more involved in care assessment for hospital patients.

People from independent sector agencies were increasingly involved (Table 4.1). For example, staff from voluntary or private residential and nursing homes often visited to assess the suitability of a patient for their particular home. These staff are now major 'stakeholders' in care assessment, since the independent sector (particularly commercial nursing homes) has grown substantially and by 1996 accounted for 80 per cent of total provision (Audit Commission 1997: 14). Multiple assessment for residential and nursing home placements warrants further study since it appears to duplicate some hospital-based assessment and may contribute to discharge delays.

## Multidisciplinary assessment

The consensus is that multidisciplinary assessment is an essential component of hospital elderly care medicine although it is not clear what this means in practice. This study used several

**Table 4.3** Multidisciplinary assessment

| *Procedures* | *Hospitals per cent* |
|---|---|
| Multiple nursing home assess (5+ staff) | 69 (N = 54) |
| Multiple community assess (5+ staff) | 76 (N = 54) |
| All patients discussed in ward meetings | 64 (N = 52) |
| All patients get social services assessment | 30 (N = 53) |
| Social services assess 'complex' cases | 98 (N = 54) |
| Social worker does not do NHS assessment | 57 (N = 53) |

measures in order to examine the extent to which multidisciplinary assessment was common practice. The first measure, the involvement score, discussed earlier, showed that a complex case assessment always involved at least five types of staff in the majority of hospitals. Five-plus staff were involved assessing nursing home cases in nearly 70 per cent of hospitals, and in assessing complex community care cases in over three-quarters of hospitals (Table 4.3).

The ward meeting was taken as another measure since this is the main multidisciplinary forum. Social workers in 64 per cent of hospitals said that all patients were reviewed in the ward meeting. A ward meeting offers all professionals an opportunity to put their views, although discussion on each patient takes, on average, less than five minutes. (Staff in the three selected patient review hospitals were asked how many patients were discussed in ward meetings and how long the meetings lasted.)

Another indicator to multidisciplinary assessment is the proportion of patients who are assessed by social services. In 30 per cent of hospitals every person admitted to elderly care wards was formally assessed by social services staff. An automatic assessment by social services, therefore, was a minority, not majority, pattern. This suggests that a screening procedure is in place in most hospitals in order to identify patients who are to be referred to social services.

Multidisciplinary assessment was undertaken with most patients regarded as having 'complex' needs – which in practice mostly meant needing an expensive package of services. In virtually all these hospitals (98 per cent), social services assessed all 'complex' cases. Multidisciplinary assessment can also mean multiple assessment, which can be problematic. A hospital is a confusing place for patients, who are seen by many staff in the course of their treatment. Some social workers in this survey said that too many people assessed patients. 'Patients see so many staff as it is. One patient I visited had seen fourteen different staff in one day' (Hospital 67). Multiple assessment can be annoying for patients. 'Patients are "assessed to death". By the time we (social services) get involved they have been asked the same questions by several staff and feel they have said it all before' (Hospital 20). Not all patients in elderly care wards were assessed automatically by social services staff, therefore, in 70 per cent of hospitals. The following types of patient were regarded as not needing a multidisciplinary assessment.

*No post-hospital care needs:* Social services respondents thought that fewer people got care assessments on acute care wards with a rapid turnover – although many perhaps did not need post-hospital assistance. This proportion is unknown since this study concentrated upon elderly care units. (The proportion referred for care assessment in the patient review in three elderly care units is examined in Chapter 8.)

*Simple community care cases:* An unknown proportion of patients in some hospitals were referred directly by the ward nurse to the area social services team, not the hospital social services team, for an assessment (since they needed only a short-term simple service or were already current clients).

*NHS continuing health care:* Social workers in 57 per cent of hospitals said that they were not always involved in assessing patients for NHS continuing health care: whether long-stay hospital beds, NHS fully funded nursing home beds, or community health services (Table 4.3). These were seen as 'medical' cases, since the NHS was responsible for 'continuing care'. One social worker respondent explained that the doctor must sign the report recommending NHS continuing care (usually written by the social worker). A doctor's signature is usually not required if the SSD is to provide or purchase nursing home care, but in practice a doctor's opinion is always sought (Hospital 30). This team, therefore, practised multipdisciplinary assessment when considering a placement for institutional care – whether NHS or SSD funded. Although the social services department is the 'lead agency' for community care under the 1990 NHS and Community Care Act, this role does not extend to community health care. These cases were assessed by the consultant, ward nursing staff, the physical therapists, a hospital discharge manager or nursing home liaison (usually positions held by nurses), or by a district nurse liaison. This suggests that involvement by social services in assessment was often in their role as purchaser rather than as a contributor to a multidisciplinary perspective.

*Self funding patients:* Some social services teams did not assess 'self funding' patients who, according to ward staff, could afford to pay for their own post-hospital community or institutional care (for example, Hospitals 46, 54, 67). This again suggests that these social services staff were involved in assessment in their purchaser role, not for their contribution to a 'holistic' assessment. As this question was not systematically asked in the survey, it is not clear whether it is a widespread SSD policy to only assess patients where the SSD might be called upon to pay.

*Rejected SSD referrals:* Social services respondents said that they did not necessarily assess everyone referred for assistance. They were only obliged under the 1990 NHS and Community Care Act to assess people who 'need' services, which can be interpreted as those who fit eligibility criteria. Some social workers followed up virtually all referrals with an 'initial' assessment, some thought about half of referrals were assessed, while others mentioned varying proportions. This question could not be pursued, since few hospital social services teams maintained statistical data on rejected referrals. Intake decisions were often made on the basis of referral information from the ward nurse. The rejected referrals were regarded as ineligible, 'inappropriate', or low priority. Referrals were considered in the light of SSD eligibility criteria, priority groups, and the funds left in the budget (although the latter criterion has been the subject of court cases).

## Staff assessment time

Assessment that involves several types of staff, and perhaps lengthy procedures, clearly can be expensive in terms of staff time. The time taken on care assessment has been little researched, since reliable estimates of staff time are difficult to obtain (Netten & Dennet 1997). Staff in two selected hospital teams were asked to estimate the time taken on a list of care assessment tasks to the nearest quarter hour. The results of this small sample indicate some differences between types of assessment and types of staff. It should be noted that this is not the total cost of an assessment, since more staff are usually involved in 'complex' community care and also institutional care assessments. The following staff were interviewed in person or by telephone: ward nurse, occupational therapist, and the ward social worker. The hourly costs for these three types of staff are fairly similar, so that the main cost differential is the time spent on care assessment. Staff were asked about typical cases, assessed in the previous week or so, in relation to four types of care assessments: assessment for district nursing (done by ward nurse or district nurse liaison); nursing home (joint SSD/NHS assessment); SSD home care only (simple – below SSD case ceiling budget amount); SSD multiple community services (complex or expensive).

At a minimum, these staff discuss each case in a ward meeting. Otherwise estimates vary considerably between staff for the time spent on similar care assessment tasks (Table 4.7). For example, the ward nurse in Team A, where the nurses act as a link and are veiy active in care assessment, spent over 19 hours assessing a patient for a nursing home placement, while the social worker spent over 14 hours and the occupational therapist nearly four hours. At a minimum, Team A staff costs for a nursing home assessment were £523. This sounds costly but amounts to less than two weeks in a residential or nursing home: the weekly unit cost of a private sector residential care home was £267, and a private nursing home was £410 (Netten & Dennett 1996: 67–69).

A simple assessment in Team C (a minimum estimate) would cost at least £179 in staff time. (The occupational therapy assessment covers a home visit for a new patient.) This is slightly more costly than a standard one-week package of domiciliary care at the SSD budget ceiling of £150.

It might be less expensive, therefore, to allocate a short-term package of care to vulnerable older people being discharged home and review the situation after one week. The ward nurse could screen, do a basic assessment, and check the service decision at the ward meeting. Some hospital 'after care' schemes follow this procedure (for example, Hospital 60, page 39). The counter arguments are that a comprehensive assessment ensures that only 'needy' people get services (a 'needs-led' principle), that appropriate services are arranged, that the minimum necessary services are arranged (rationing), and that client outcomes are better.

## Summary

Two key findings emerge from this overview of care assessment in hospital elderly care units. First, patterns of care assessment in terms of staffing and task allocations were complex, since many permutations are possible. Second, multidisciplinary assessment was regarded as best practice and was also common practice, at least for patients regarded as having multiple post-hospital needs for assistance. Ten staff usually were involved in assessing complex cases. In three-quarters of teams, five staff always assessed patients needing a community care package or residential or nursing home care. These staff were the social worker/care manager, nurse, consultant/geriatrician, occupational therapist and physiotherapist. General practitioners were notable for their absence from post-hospital care decisions. Nearly two-thirds of elderly care teams reviewed all patients in ward meetings. Multidisciplinary assessment therefore was a considerable investment in staff time in cases where older patients needed long term care, the rationale being that this was worthwhile in humanitarian and financial terms.

The purpose of a formal care assessment in many hospitals, however, was seen as service gatekeeping, not as 'best practice' holistic assessment of older patients. Four groups of patients did not necessarily receive a multidisciplinary assessment, being seen only by the organisation that was to fund the service. First, those thought not to need post-hospital assistance usually were not formally assessed. Second, in one-third of teams the geriatrician was not always involved where patients were going home with social services. Third, social services in over half of hospitals did not assess patients discharged to NHS continuing health care. Fourth, social services did not necessarily assess where patients were 'self funding'.

Care assessment was a contested function in 'simple' cases since each occupational group believed that they could assess the need for standard services. Geriatricians saw themselves as the leader of the elderly care team and most decisions were mediated through the multidisciplinary ward meeting chaired by the consultant. Nurses have expanded their jurisdiction in care assessment procedures and some had been appointed to formal assessment positions. Occupational therapists played a major role in assessing whether an older person could manage in their home environment. Social workers regarded themselves as the 'lead' workers in care assessment.

5

# Care Assessment Procedures

The previous chapter examined who does care assessments while this chapter examines in more detail how care assessment is done. The procedures involved in assessing patients for discharge to post-hospital care are identified and discussed using a patient flowchart as a framework. This 'task oriented' framework sets out the key tasks, decision points and designated staff. One way of analysing team functioning is in terms of client/patient pathways and the decisions required from team members at each point (Øvretveit 1997). This approach was familiar to staff since it was used in guidance documents on discharge (Department of Health 1989b, 1995b), in the *Hospital Discharge Workbook* (Department of Health 1994), and is set out in hospital discharge protocols. Care assessment can be defined as an ongoing patient pathway that covers eligibility screening, referral, diagnosis/assessment, consultation, service planning, and discharge.

The telephone survey of social workers in 54 hospital elderly care teams asked them in detail about who did what and when. This is supplemented by material from the visits to ten hospitals: interviews with health care professionals and an examination of standard forms.

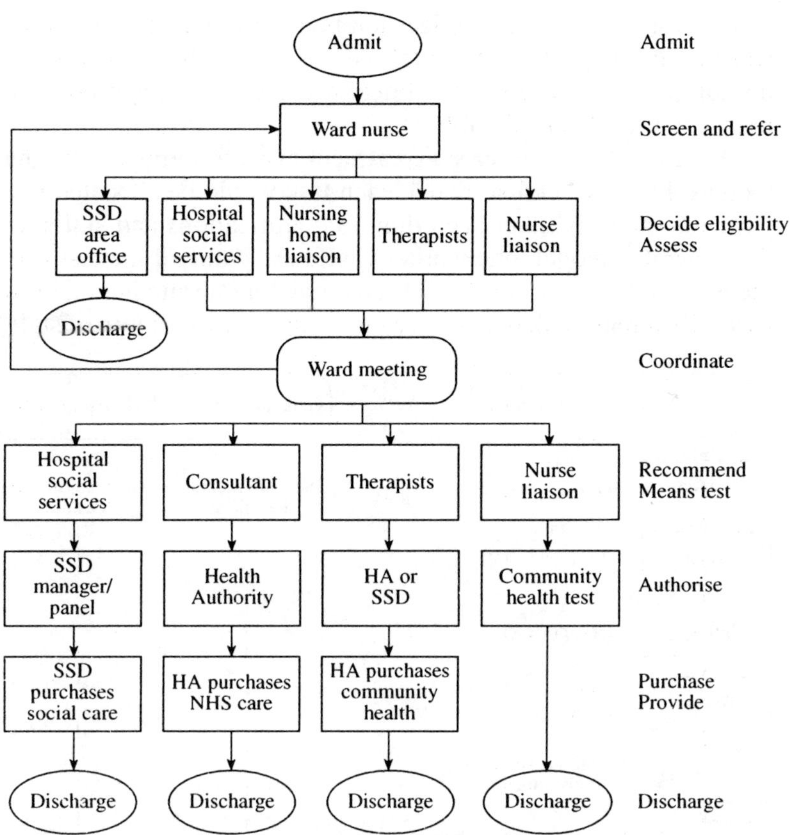


**Figure 5.1** Patient flowchart: care assessment decision points

## Patient pathways

Efforts to improve work performance in hospitals, in terms of effectiveness and efficiency, have adopted elements of organizational 're-engineering' and the application of 'patient-focused' care (Walston and Kimberley 1997). This generally involves determining who is responsible for what tasks in relation to patients, and setting out the procedures for completing these tasks.

Figure 5.1 sets out a patient flowchart with stages identified during interviews with health and social services staff. A series of care assessment stages and decision points from admission to the ward to discharge from hospital were traced, although decisions do not always proceed in the linear order depicted, and hospital practices varied considerably.

Figure 5.2 sets out care assessment tasks in terms of staffing models. In the specialist model, each task would be allocated to a particular staff member according to qualifications and skills. In the generalist model, one worker would carry out all the tasks. In the multiskill model, staff could substitute for one another on most tasks. Different models would require a different skill mix of staff.

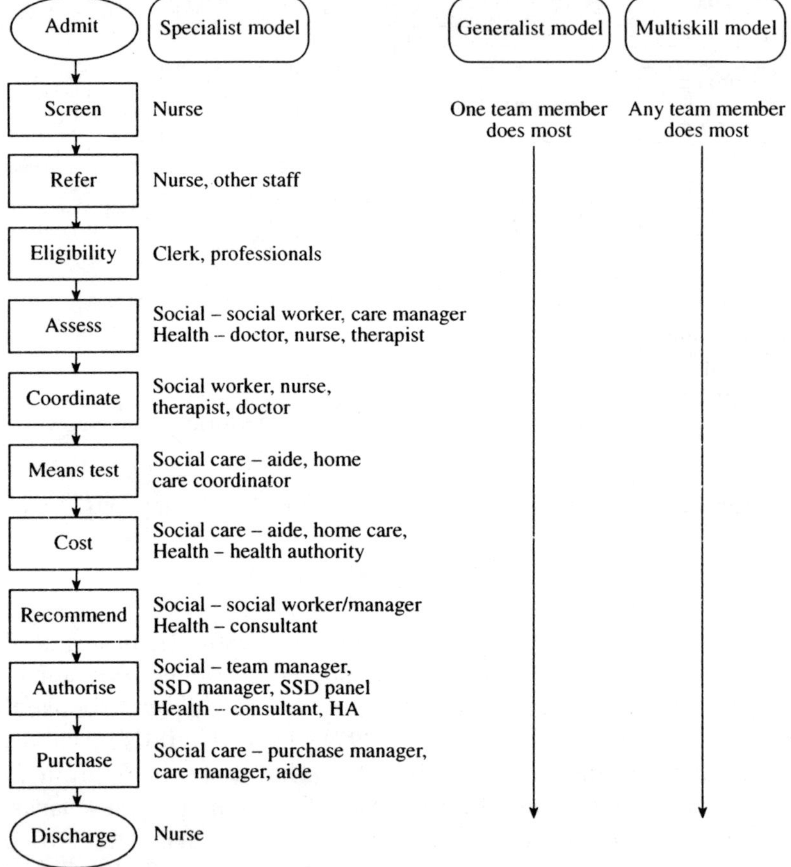


**Figure 5.2** Team models: care assessment tasks

## Screening procedures

Hospital elderly care teams pay particular attention to screening and referral since there is pressure to identify people early in their hospital stay who need services arranged before they can be discharged. A referral is an important decision point since this often predicts whether an elderly patient goes home upon discharge or enters institutional care (Centre for Health Services Research 1996).

The pressure upon hospital beds means that referrals have to be earlier and more systematic. Hospitals have been urged to set up procedures so that referrals are made in plenty of time to plan for discharge (Department of Health 1994; Audit Commission 1997: 18). The expectation based on other studies was that the ward nurse would screen patients for referral for a care assessment (Social Services Inspectorate 1995).

In 56 per cent of hospitals, the discharge protocol specified a formal screening procedure and designated a particular member of staff as responsible for screening patients likely to need assistance upon discharge (Table 5.1). This was mostly the ward nurse (Table 5.2). The 'named nurse' screened patients within 24 hours of admission using a standard form with 'trigger questions' for referrals, such as whether the person was coping at home (for example, Hospital 8). Ward nurses had to make an early judgement on a patient's likely need for assistance and then stream patients into assessment channels that led to certain services. This provoked some 'culture clash'. Social services and occupational therapy staff said that doctors and nurses tried to 'short cut' the assessment process by specifying in the referral the service needs of patients rather than waiting for an assessment. Social services staff interpreted the 1990 NHS and Community Care Act to mean that an assessment should precede a service decision, that is, that assessment should be 'needs-led'. In all hospitals, referrals also were made later during the patient's stay in hospital and by other staff, and the ward meeting was an important forum for referrals in over half of hospitals (Table 5.1).

The majority pattern in these hospital elderly care units was a formal screening procedure and a multidiscipinary assessment where a patient had multiple needs. Some hospitals, however,

**Table 5.1** Assessment decision points

| *Decision points* | *Teams* |
|---|---|
| Formal screening | 56% (N=54) |
| Ward meeting referrals | 52% (N=54) |
| Formal coordination | 66% (N=53) |
| Ward meeting | 90% (N=52) |

routed care assessment to different staff. In one hospital, social services staff were not actively involved, which appeared to be associated with the non-availability of SSD services.

## Patient eligibility for social services

Hospital social services teams had to make two decisions on patient eligibility for SSD resources. First, whether to accept a referral (an intake decision), and second, whether (after a formal assessment) to allocate resources. The 'intake' decision involved deciding whether a person's needs and level of priority made them potentially eligible for assistance. Hospital social services teams had different procedures for deciding whether to accept a referral. The intake decision was usually made by the ward social worker, in some hospitals by the team manager (Hospital 11), or in an 'intake team' meeting each morning (Hospital 42). These intake decisions were based upon broad SSD eligibility criteria, as discussed later. Social workers in some hospitals said that a large (but unknown) proportion of referrals were refused. Statistics were not routinely kept by all hospital social services teams on whether referrals were refused or accepted.

## Care assessment practice

Assessment practices differed considerably between different hospital elderly care units, different staff and different patients. Assessment can range from one procedure undertaken by one staff member to a series of assessments made by several staff over several

**Table 5.2** Responsible staff members

| *Staff member* | *Teams* |
|---|---|
| Nurse screens and refers | 80% (N=36) |
| Social worker does only 'complex' assessment | 18% (N=54) |
| Social worker coordinates assessment | 39% (N=36) |
| Nurse coordinates assessment | 40% (N=36) |
| SSD manager/team leader recommends complex social services | 66% (N=53) |
| SSD panel/manager authorises complex social services | 34% (N=52) |
| Consultant authorises NHS services | 65% (N=53) |

weeks. Staff might base an assessment upon a quick observation, a lengthy interview, or standardised tests of physical and cognitive functioning such as Barthel Scales (Royal College of Physicians & British Geriatrics Society 1992). An assessment opinion might be given verbally, on a standard form, in a written note, or in a full report. For example, occupational therapists emphasised the importance of assessing a person in their home environment.

Several occupational groups claimed competence in assessing the need for assistance in relatively straightforward cases. 'Simple' cases were variously assessed by social workers, social services aides, ex-home organisers, nurses and occupational therapists. A 'simple' care assessment was contested territory and work practices differed across hospitals. For example, some ward nurses saw their screening interview as an assessment, while social services staff regarded it as a referral.

*Simple and complex care assessment:* Social services teams commonly divided patients into 'simple' and 'complex' cases for assessment purposes and this terminology was also used by other staff. This division was not clear cut. It depended upon the number of services (one service usually was defined as a 'simple' assessment), the type of service (residential and nursing home care was a complex assessment), the level of need (multiple needs were higher priority than single needs), whether a new case or a current

## Hospital 51

The hospital is based on the outskirts of a northern town. The elderly care unit had several wards. Post-hospital care was in crisis since the SSD had overspent its budget and expensive services were not being authorised. The named nurse screened and referred patients. Ward meetings were chaired by the ward nurse manager or consultant, and assessment and discharge were coordinated at this meeting. Case conferences were held for difficult cases. Only a minority of cases were referred to social services staff prior to discharge. The named nurse was designated as coordinator for NHS continuing care cases. The physiotherapist and occupational therapist attended ward rounds and assessed most rehabilitation patients.

client (who only needed a service 'restart'), the cost of care (expensive services were 'complex' and required a higher level of authorisation), and the level of dependency (patients who required services in order to be discharged were high priority). These cases called for different procedures and forms, and were sometimes assigned to different staff. In nearly 20 per cent of the 54 hospitals, social workers did not do 'simple' assessments, which were handled by other accredited 'assessors' including home care organisers (Table 5.2). These hospital social services teams followed a specialist model of working with differentiated tasks assigned to different staff (see Hospital 25).

## Coordinating care assessment

Care assessment clearly can be a complex procedure, especially for patients with multiple needs, since it can involve up to ten staff. In two-thirds of hospitals, someone was formally designated to coordinate the care assessment procedure (Table 5.1). This was the hospital social worker in nearly 40 per cent of hospitals and the nurse in about one-third (Table 5.2). In other hospitals responsibility for coordinating assessment was often seen as split between 'health' aspects and 'social' aspects, and hence split or shared between the nurse and the social worker.

## Hospital 27

The Trust managed two hospitals in a Midlands city. The elderly care unit was located in the rehabilitation hospital with over 100 acute and rehabilitation beds. Post-discharge care health and social care were adequate. Procedures were formal and standardised.

The nurse screened and referred on a standard form and coordinated the assessment process. All staff attended ward meetings, which discussed most patients. Forms were numerous and repetitive with considerable duplication. Occupational therapists made home visits, often accompanied by the social services home care organiser. Social services followed a specialist model, with 'simple' assessments done by the home care organiser and 'complex' assessments by the social worker.

Ward meetings were the main forum for coordinating staff activities in relation to referrals, assessment, service decisions, and discharges. Weekly meetings were held in 90 per cent of hospitals, often following the ward round, and were attended by most staff (Table 5.1).

About one-third of hospitals also held separate 'care planning' meetings which the consultants did not attend. In a few hospitals, the consultant only attended ward rounds and relayed any views on post-hospital care services through the nurse manager (for example, Hospital 59). Social workers seldom attended ward rounds, which were the province of doctors and nurses.

Ward meeting procedures depend to a large extent on the consultant. One social worker respondent said that one consultant conducted discussions at the foot of the patient's bed, while another kept the ward round to medical matters and the staff all held a multidisciplinary meeting afterwards.

Case conferences convened to discuss particular cases were no longer a regular procedure. A few hospitals held these about once a month on elderly care wards, convened by the nurse ward manager or social worker. Case conferences were frequent in only one hospital. The social worker said there were about nine per week across the whole hospital, chaired by the social services team leader and lasting about one hour. Social services called these for complicated cases and for all nursing home cases, Doctors were invited but did not attend, and relayed their opinions through nurses. The 'primary nurse' usually attended and other nurses 'popped in' to give their views. The patient always attended (unless there was severe dementia) and family members were invited to attend (Hospital 17).

## Authorising post-hospital services

The health and social services professionals in the elderly care team generally could not allocate or purchase post-hospital assistance for their patients without approval by management. In the case of social services, team managers – not care managers – controlled funds, as explained below, so that the team social worker had little power over resources.

*Social services:* Social services respondents in 54 hospitals were asked who authorised social services resources. There was no simple answer. Most social services departments had set case level budget ceilings which involved four linked factors: time, cost, service type, and provider type. The time frame typically was up to 4 or 6 weeks post-discharge; a ceiling was set upon the weekly cost of the client package; this ceiling varied with the type of service (community or institutional); and distinctions were made between SSD (in-house) and independent sector services. The domiciliary budget ceiling usually was set below the cost of a residential home placement. The level of authorisation rose with the cost of services. The SSD area manager or an SSD panel mostly authorised community services above the budget ceiling, and authorised all residential or nursing home cases. The decision-making chain also distinguished between recommendation and authorisation.

The recommendation by the social worker had to be approved by the hospital social services team manager in about half of hospitals for short-term services, and in about two-thirds of hospitals for longer term services (Table 5.2). Social workers authorised short-term domiciliary services in only 14 per cent of hospitals, while in 46 per cent the team managers authorised services purchases and the SSD area office in the remaining 40 per cent. Virtually all complex packages (expensive services and residential or nursing home places) were authorised by the team leader or by a SSD panel. Nearly 40 per cent of hospital social services teams did not have a devolved budget and all decisions were made by the SSD area team manager, especially where patients were discharged from hospital to an area care manager (Table 5.2). These findings are in line with those of the Audit Commission (1997: 34), which reported that in a sample of local authorities only one-sixth of frontline care managers were budget-holders and then usually only for limited services.

*NHS continuing care:* The consultant authorised NHS continuing care in 65 per cent of these hospitals (Table 5.2), although expensive cases generally went to a health authority manager or panel. Other studies report that consultants believe that they have less power over continuing health decisions under the new policies (Centre for Health Services Research 1996). This was also the view of consultants interviewed in the ten hospitals.

*Aids and equipment:* Occupational therapists arranged equipment from different suppliers and practices varied between local areas. Aids and equipment were loaned or bought from different sources: some hospital occupational therapy departments had their own hospital store or shared with nursing; the main source was the SSD equipment store; other sources included community nursing, voluntary organisations such as Red Cross, or private providers such as pharmacies.

## Costing and purchasing services

The implementation from 1993 onwards of case-level purchasing responsibilities had introduced a new set of tasks for social services such as costing services, means assessment, and purchasing of care packages. Patients were means tested as to their capacity to pay for SSD community and institutional care, using a detailed financial assessment form. The task of financial assessment was carried out by aides in some hospital teams but by care managers/social workers in most. A common assessment and purchase staffing split was for ex-home care organisers or social services aides to arrange services once authorisation was received. For example, in a specialist team, 'paper walls' were erected between care assessors who assessed, the team manager who recommended services, and staff who means-tested, costed and organised services (Hospitals 32, 44); other hospital teams did only assessment and costing while the area SSD office purchased (for example, Hospital 44).

### Arranging discharges

Discharge arrangements were handled, as was long-standing practice, by the named nurse or the ward nurse manager. This involved sorting out medication, making outpatient appointments, arranging transport, filling out discharge forms, and sending referral information to district nurses and GP practice nurses. In the ten hospitals visited, the consultant sent a standard letter to the patient's GP; common practice in most hospitals (Closs 1997).

## Formal procedures

There is a long history of efforts to promote cooperation between health and social services on hospital discharge arrangements (see for example, Department of Health 1989b). During the 1990s, the Department of Health began to require, not just urge, agreements between local health and social services authorities. Social services department from December 1992 onwards (the 31 December agreement) were required to reach agreements with local health authorities as a pre-condition for payment of the community care special transitional grant (Department of Health, Local Authority Social Services Letter 1992). The Department of Health also published 'best practice' guidelines recommending formal procedures in order to promote more effective teamwork (Department of Health 1994). Social services respondents were asked in this survey (N = 54) whether discharge protocols and eligibility guidelines (that superseded the early requirements) had been implemented.

## Hospital discharge protocols

Social services department and local health authorities were required to produce written statements on jointly agreed assessment and hospital discharge procedures and to make these available to patients by 29 September 1995 (Department of Health 1995b). This hospital discharge protocol was to set out the decision points, who was responsible, how the task would be done, and how long it would take. Social workers in the 54 hospitals were asked (one year after the implementation date) whether a discharge protocol had been produced in their hospital.

These were available in most hospitals since 78 per cent of respondents used these published procedures, 13 per cent said they were in draft form, while 9 per cent had not seen any documentation (Table 5.3). Social workers generally were positive about these protocols, which they thought had improved interprofessional working and discharge practices. For example, they had grounds to complain if older patients were discharged hastily in violation of written policy before community services were arranged. Some hospitals specified time standards which put more pressure upon social services to expedite discharge arrangements, usually with a few days for a single service and about two weeks for a complex service package. The Audit Commission (1997: 22) found that only two out of eleven social services departments in their field study had agreed times in place for all processes (referral to case intake, referral to completed assessment, and assessment to care package in place), and that these time periods varied considerably.

## NHS eligibility criteria

Health authorities and social services departments were required to produce respective eligibility criteria and to clarify their joint responsibilities in draft form by 30 September 1995 and in final published form by 1 April 1996 (Dept of Health 1995b). Social services respondents were asked about the criteria for NHS responsibilities for continuing health care which were due three months prior the telephone survey. Eligibility criteria had been

**Table 5.3** Formal procedures

| *Formal procedures* | *Hospitals per cent* |
|---|---|
| Published hospital discharge protocols | 78 (N = 54) |
| Published health authority criteria | 76 (N = 54) |
| Published SSD criteria | 89 (N = 54) |
| SSD care plan – always written | 76 (N = 54) |

published by their health authority and were being used in 76 per cent of these hospitals, while another 17 per cent were still in draft form, and had not been produced in the remaining 8 per cent (Table 5.3). Agreement had not been reached at the time of the survey, therefore, in about one-quarter of hospitals. For example, one health authority was working on its fifth draft (Hospital 30). These disagreements were about cost-shifting, since SSD managers believed that the impact would be a large shift in responsibility from the NHS to local authority social services (for example, Hospitals 31, 35, 53). For example, one SSD director had issued a statement that the SSD would not fund nursing home placements for terminally ill people (Hospital 60).

Social services respondents described variations on an 'NHS banding scheme' of between three and six bands, which categorised patients in terms of respective health and social services responsibilities and level of priority. Henwood (1996) found considerable variation among 25 health authorities in how they defined eligibility for NHS care, including descriptions of medical conditions, intensity of need, and measures of dependency. One of our social services respondents explained that the consultant decided where a person fits on a broad three-category NHS 'banding scheme' after discussion at the ward meeting:

> *'Band 1 equals a very dependent patient who is a continuing case NHS responsibility; band 2 equals mixed needs so that the patient is a joint NHS and SSD responsibility; and band 3 is social care so that the patient is the responsibility of the SSD after discharge from hospital' (Hospital 32).*

## SSD eligibility criteria

Social workers in nearly 90 per cent of hospitals said that the SSD had published eligibility criteria, while the remainder were in draft form or had not yet been produced (Table 5.3). Some SSDs had incorporated the NHS banding scheme in their eligibility criteria: 5 = total nursing care, 4 = residential or complex at home package, 3 = medium dependency, 2 = less dependent, 1 = single service (for example, Hospital 7). 'Risk' was an important concept since the guidance *NHS Responsibilities* (Department of Health 1995b) implies that the NHS cannot unilaterally discharge people from hospital to community care if the SSD states that the discharge is not safe. SSDs varied in how eligibility was defined and the degree of specificity but the highest priority went to those deemed to be 'at risk'. One respondent explained:

> *'Only people deemed to be at serious risk get help, while prevention or maintenance are very low priority. Category 1 are people whose problems make them a risk to themselves or others or who would worsen markedly without help. This is the high priority group who have first call on our help. Category 2 may become a risk. Category 3 are not having severe difficulties although help would prevent any difficulties getting worse' (Hospital 33).*

## Standard forms

Social services respondents in the telephone survey were asked whether standard forms were used. Examples of standard forms in relation to care assessment were also collected in the ten hospitals visited. As explained below, communications between members of the hospital elderly care team had become increasingly formal, at least in relation to the key decision points along the assessment pathway. A few hospitals, however, had retained informal working arrangements (see Hospital 67, overleaf).

*Referral form:* A specific question was not asked in the telephone survey but a standard form appeared to be a common practice. In

## Hospital 67

This typical district hospital located in a market town provided the usual spectrum of acute care. Staff said that post-hospital community and institutional resource were inadequate, and the SSD had overspent its budget. The elderly care wards were separate from the main hospital but on the same site which highlights the separation of elderly care from the rest of 'acute' health care. The multidisciplinary team communicated informally with few standard forms and little written information. The named nurse screened, referred, and coordinated the 'health' aspects of care assessment. All staff attended the weekly ward meeting where all patients were discussed and care decisions made. The social worker undertook the 'social care' assessment but also believed that she coordinated the whole assessment process rather than the named nurses who were seldom on duty at the crucial time.

eight out of the ten hospitals visited, social services insisted on a formal referral and no longer accepted a 'coffee break referral'. Referrals were systematically updated by the ward nurse on a referral form in the patient medical record in the ten hospitals visited. Formal procedures identified in the telephone interviews included referring through the hospital computer system (Hospital 30); telephoning the social services office 'intake coordinator' who filled in a form (Hospitals 17, 53); while some social services teams only accepted referrals during certain hours. For example, the social services team in Hospital 37 took telephone referrals all day Monday but only on afternoons the rest of the week; in Hospital 7 telephone referrals were only accepted in the mornings. The exceptions to this formality were elderly care units with a strong team ethos where the social worker visited the ward every day and 'knew everyone' (Hospitals 1, 32, 38, 46). Social services respondents thought that a formal referral procedure was desirable: it regulated workloads, discouraged low priority referrals, and allowed the monitoring of performance targets. Some other hospital staff, however, were irritated by standard forms and restricted referral hours: one geriatrician described this as 'the social services bureaucracy gone mad'.

*Standard assessment form:* In the ten hospitals visited, occupational groups mainly filled out their own forms, resulting in considerable duplication. Only one hospital used a joint care assessment form for all health professionals, but this did not include a section for the social worker. The different professions in these ten hospital teams all used different assessment categories. Further, these varied across hospitals. This lack of comparability limited the data that could be collected in the patient case notes review stage of our study. Other studies have also commented on the lack of standardised measures. Shared multidisciplinary assessment notes in hospitals are rare, since multidisciplinary team members have not managed to agree upon standard measures of need (Centre for Health Services Research 1996; Closs 1997; Caldock 1996: 29). Further, social services departments do not use standard measures, so that no comparison can be made across local authorities on which clients receive what services and why (Carpenter & Calnan 1997).

*Patient care plan:* The expectation in official guidelines is that a care plan is drawn up listing the services that a person will receive upon discharge. Patients should leave hospital with a written copy setting out all services that have been arranged, the dates of appointments, and the key people and their telephone numbers (Department of Health 1994; Audit Commission 1997: 18). We found various nursing care plans, social services care plans, and discharge plans. None of the ten hospitals visited had a joint care plan that went home with the patient as a single document. The closest was a discharge form lodged in the patient medical record that stated what post-hospital care arrangements had been made. The SSD care plan was a separate document. Over three-quarters of social workers in the telephone survey said that a written care plan was produced in complex cases, but not necessarily in simple cases (Table 5.3). This care plan was primarily a purchasing document for staff, however, and with few exceptions was not seen by the patient. The SSD care plans in the ten hospitals were daunting-looking technical forms. No summary of the SSD care plan was lodged in the patient medical record, which was a wasted opportunity for better communication with hospital staff.

## Summary

Most hospital elderly care teams (N = 54) identified care assessment stages and the staff member responsible in a process that could involve ten staff and a chain of decision-making. Patients were screened by a ward nurse in half these hospitals and the ward meeting was a common forum for referrals between staff. Work practices differed considerably across hospitals on 'simple' care cases, being variously assessed by social workers, social services aides, ex-home organisers, nurses and occupational therapists. Complex cases generally were assessed by social workers. A designated person, usually the social worker, was responsible for coordinating care assessment in two-thirds of elderly care teams, but 'health' and 'social' aspects were often separately coordinated. Elderly care team members had little control over post-hospital services. Managers, not team members, authorised social services budgets. For example, less than one in five hospital social workers could authorise short term post-hospital assistance and all residential and nursing home recommendations went to managers or SSD panels for decisions.

Procedures had become more formal as required in a series of Department of Health guidelines during the 1990s. This survey of 54 elderly care hospital teams (in July 1996) showed that most had instituted formal procedures. About 80 per cent of health authorities had published eligibility criteria for NHS continuing care; 90 per cent of social services departments had published eligibility criteria; and nearly 80 per cent of hospitals had published discharge protocols. Standard forms were used in many hospitals. The ten hospitals visited used an admission screening form, a written referral to social services, and a discharge form listing the arranged health and social services. The different disciplines still filled out separate care assessment forms, however, with considerable information overlap.

Care assessment processes, therefore, have become more formal, transparent and standardised. Within this overall pattern, however, there is considerable variability in how care assessment procedures are carried out across hospital elderly care teams. The next chapter explores whether staff regarded the trend to greater formality in work practices as an improvement.

# 6

# Better Assessment

Theories of interorganisational and interprofessional behaviour predict that collaboration is difficult to achieve (Perrow 1986). The literature on collaboration between health and social services stretches back for decades in many countries and is replete with exhortations for staff to work better together despite the many barriers (see for example, Hokenstad & Ritvo 1982). In the UK, the health and social services sectors have been urged to produce a seamless service in organising community care (Audit Commission 1992a). The normative expectation should be, therefore, that hospital elderly care teams will find collaborating on care assessment difficult rather than easy, since they work across the division between health and social services sectors, involve several agencies, and contain staff from different disciplines.

Effective teamwork in the health and social services has been much studied (for example, Qualls & Czirr 1988; Lonsdale et al 1980; Alexander et al 1992; Poulton & West 1993a,1993b). Øvretveit et al (1997) identify team integration as an important dimension since teams may be tightly or loosely knit. The types of integration factors relevant to hospital elderly care teams are whether they meet regularly, whether all members assess all patients, and whether they take separate or collective decisions. Headrick et al (1998) have culled a list of attributes from the research literature that are associated with effective interprofessional teamwork in health care. These include a shared mission/values, mutual support between staff, member roles are agreed and clear, tasks are defined and achievable, members participate in team decisions, and there are clear management and information structures. These attributes can be grouped under two main dimensions: team integration (tight or loosely knit teams), and formality (formal or informal team procedures).

This chapter presents the views of social workers in 54 hospital elderly care teams on whether care assessment was better under the post-1990 NHS and Community Care policies and procedures. The relationship between better care assessment and dimensions such as team integration, formality, and multidisciplinary assessment are investigated.

## Social work opinions

Social services staff in the hospital elderly care teams were asked their opinion, during telephone interviews (in July 1996), on whether the care assessment of older patients was better, the same, or worse since the implementation of the 1990 NHS and Community Care Act (from 1993 onwards). Their opinions are significant, since these were experienced staff, based in 54 large acute care hospitals, and were employed by nearly half the social services departments in England. Since most respondents had a social work qualification, their views represent an occupational group as well as an organisational view. Their opinions are shown in Tables 6.1 and 6.2. Figure 6.1 juxtaposes some key findings (for example, better assessments, less job satisfaction).

**Table 6.1** Opinions on care assessment quality

| *Opinions* | *Quality of assessment (N = 54)* | *Patient outcomes (N = 54)* | *Relations with staff (N = 54)* | *Relations with patient (N = 51)* |
|---|---|---|---|---|
| Better | 89% | 70% | 54% | 22% |
| Same | 6% | 4% | 24% | 28% |
| Worse | 6% | 9% | 15% | 39% |
| Don't know | – | 17% | 7% | 11% |

**Table 6.2** Opinions on care assessment procedures

| *Opinions* | *Assessment time (N = 54)* | *Staff involved (N = 54)* | *Job satisfaction (N = 54)* |
|---|---|---|---|
| More | 78% | 65% | 13% |
| Same | 9% | 15% | 20% |
| Less | 9% | 13% | 59% |
| Don't know | 4% | 7% | 7% |

## Was the quality of assessment better?

Most hospital social workers (nearly 90 per cent) reported that overall the quality of care assessment was better. The reasons given for this judgement were that a formal care assessment was being done for more people, assessment was more comprehensive, procedures were clearer, assessment forms were standardised, and assessment had a clear purpose. The few who thought it worse, only 6 per cent, said that assessment was too rushed, and concentrated upon a person's practical needs while ignoring emotional needs.

## Were patient outcomes better?

The majority of social workers, 70 per cent, thought that outcomes for patients in terms of the services received were improved. The positive factors mentioned were intensive services for people with multiple needs, earlier discharge home with appropriate post-hospital services, fewer admissions to institutional care, and greater choice of services from a wider range of providers. About 20 per cent did not know, or thought that little had changed, while nearly 10 per cent thought that patient outcomes were worse.

Nearly all social workers said, however, that although very dependent people got more assistance, less dependent people got little or no help. The main concern was the absence of preventive services for people who needed a small amount of short-term help. Social services department eligibility criteria generally categorised

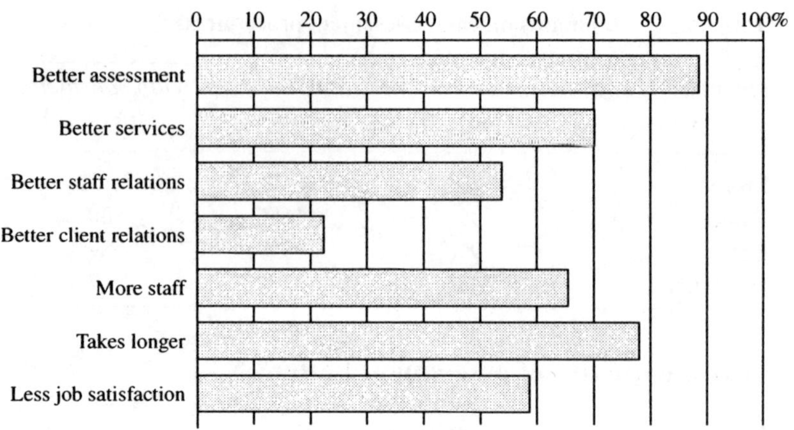


**Figure 6.1** Hospital social worker views

people with lesser 'need' as a low priority group (as explained in Chapter 5) which meant that they were unlikely to receive any post-hospital help from social services. Respondents thought that a little help for less needy people might prevent deterioration or a later crisis in a person's health or home situation. The refusal of assistance to lower dependency people often meant that families had to do more. Other negative factors cited by respondents were concern about the safety of patients discharged 'too early', families being rushed into premature decisions about institutional care, insufficient resources, and running out of funds before the end of the financial year.

The concern expressed by social workers and other 'caring professions' about the erosion of preventive services and the lack of support for people except in a crisis has also been argued in several recent reports (House of Commons 1996; Audit Commission 1997; NHS Health Advisory Service 1997; Royal Commission on Long Term Care 1999). Limited supply and rising demand have meant that the concept of prevention has been submerged. Policy priority is given to people with multiple needs who require a 'complex package of care' while people needing only single or short-term services are a low priority group. One argument in favour of prevention is that a little appropriate help early on for older people may be a cost-effective way of preventing deterioration. A second argument is that a little help can be important to older people and their family carers, who are entitled to expect a reasonable quality of life.

## Were relations with other staff better?

Over half of social workers, 54 per cent, thought that their relations with other hospital staff were better. The overall better relationship was attributed to a clearer and documented role specification for social services hospital staff. Social services staff thought that they had gained more power within the hospital, and a higher profile. Three reasons were given for this greater power. First, the 1990 NHS and Community Care Act and subsequent policies had transferred more responsibility, and hence more control, to social services departments for post-hospital social care. Second, hospital social workers were well informed and generally positive about the introduction of written hospital discharge protocols and health and social services eligibility criteria. Several commented that written guidelines strengthened their efforts to maintain good discharge practice and made it clear that social services staff would not accept responsibility if a discharge was 'not safe'. Third, other staff relied on them to interpret the stream of policy and procedural documents. Several claimed that they were the only staff in the hospital who understood the new procedures.

In hospitals where staff working relations were reported to be worse (15 per cent) social workers attributed this to cost-shifting disagreements between health and social services in the context of resource shortages. Respondents were asked how frequently (always, usually, sometimes or never) they were involved in case-level disputes over respective NHS and SSD responsibilities. About 20 per cent said that they were usually or always involved in disputes.

Some social services respondents felt that they were the 'scapegoat' for the NHS crisis since hospitals wanted to 'empty beds' and did not accept that the SSD also had resource constraints. Some difficulties in working relations were provoked by pressure from hospital managers to discharge patients as soon as they were medically fit, after which they were redefined as 'social problems', to be shifted over to social services. Several social worker respondents said that although SSD resource constraints were acknowledged, thc hospital staff think that the SSD blocks discharges. One respondent said: 'It is a myth that Social Services delays discharges, because we usually start an assessment within two days, as written into the discharge protocol. It's very seldom that delay is due to the SSD but more likely to be medical issues such as ward transfers' (Hospital 49). Most social services respondents said, however, that disagreements were at management level between the SSD and the Health Authority rather than between ward level staff. The resolution of cost-shifting disputes had escalated to management level since the members of the elderly care team (as discussed in Chapter 5) generally had little power over case-level budgets. For example, hospital social services team managers and area SSD managers were the budget holders, not the care managers.

## Were relations with clients better?

This fairly positive view of relations with other staff contrasts with the more negative view of relations with clients. Nearly 40 per cent of social workers thought that their working relationship with clients and families had grown worse in the last few years, compared to only about 20 per cent who thought that relations were better. They felt strongly about this, since social work training stresses the importance of establishing a good client–worker relationship.

The principal reasons given for a worse relationship were having to explain funding shortages, spending less time with patients and families, paying less attention to emotional than practical needs, having to do financial assessments, and dealing with cases where the house has to be sold to pay for residential or nursing home care. One social worker commented that it was very hard to explain the new NHS and SSD policies to families, and to justify helping only the most dependent people because of budget restrictions: 'I feel like piggy in the middle between families and service agencies.'

## Did assessments take more time?

Nearly 80 per cent of social workers said that each case took more time under the new procedures, but this extra time was spent on 'paperwork' rather than with patients and their families. This view was consistent with surveys of five local authorities comparing views in 1993–4 and 1995–6, which reported that 30 per cent of SSD staff said they were spending more time filling in forms (Balloch et al 1999). Formal and standardised procedures, therefore, may carry a cost in extra staff time, as does the transaction time involved in purchasing and the assessor/purchaser/provider split. Care assessment forms have to be filled out, services costed, purchase authorisation requested, financial assessments completed, and purchasing arrangements made.

## Were more staff involved in assessment?

Nearly two-thirds of respondents said that more staff were now involved in assessing the post-hospital health and social care needs of patients. Such multidisciplinary assessment was generally regarded as desirable. As shown in Chapter 4, five staff were always involved and another five usually involved in assessing people with multiple needs.

## Was job satisfaction greater?

Nearly 60 per cent of social workers reported less job satisfaction over the last few years, and only 13 per cent reported more satisfaction. This was consistent with the surveys in five local authorities (N = 1,200) where over 40 per cent of staff in the 1995–6 survey reported high stress levels (Balloch et al 1999). Apart from complaints about 'too much paperwork', the other major reason for dissatisfaction was the change in professional tasks. The social workers in our survey felt that they had lost their counselling role and had become managers, financial assessors, purchasers, 'fixers' and apologists for service shortages. They felt that other professional staff on the multidisciplinary team, in contrast, such as the geriatrician, nurse, physiotherapist and occupational therapist, had retained their treatment role with patients.

The various dissatisfactions expressed by these 54 hospital social worker respondents can be categorised in five ways. They saw themselves as 'vanishing social workers', since the numbers of social worker qualified staff had dropped relative to other-qualified staff. They were 'invisible social workers', since the social worker title had been replaced by a proliferation of other titles including care manager. They felt themselves to be 'challenged social workers', since they had lost their exclusive jurisdiction over counselling and care assessment to other professionals. They were 'changing social workers', since they had taken on resource management and care purchasing roles. They were also 'significant social workers', however, since they now had a more powerful role within the hospital as gate keepers to community care resources.

## Better teamwork

The proposition is that teams with shared goals and values and clear procedures perform the most effectively in health care settings; 'team' is a loose label, however, since these groupings vary considerably in their staffing and procedures (Øvretveit et al 1997; Headrick et al 1998). Hospital elderly care teams contain members from different professions, different employers (hospital trust, community trust and social services), and have different priorities in relation to care assessment. These divisions suggest that teams must actively seek to integrate their aims and their work practices.

The staff in the hospital elderly care teams in our survey (N = 54) met regularly and communicated on care assessment decisions verbally and in writing. Staff met in weekly ward meetings in 90 per cent of hospitals, which most staff (but not always the consultant) attended. The consultant always chaired the meetings he/she attended. Several staff commented that a hospital is a consultant-dominated system and that ward meetings were the main way for other professionals to put forward and legitimise their views. In nearly two-thirds of teams, all cases were discussed at these ward

**Table 6.3** Teamwork

| *Procedures* | *Hospital %* |
|---|---|
| Social worker attached to ward | 93 (N = 54) |
| All patients discussed in team meeting | 64 (N = 52) |
| Weekly team meetings | 90 (N = 52) |
| Social worker attends ward meetings | 92 (N = 51) |
| Social worker full member of team | 70 (N = 54) |
| Consultant charts meetings | 63 (N = 49) |

meetings – even if briefly. The division between health sector employed staff and social sector employed staff remains a large divide to be bridged within elderly care teams. The social worker said that she/he felt like a full member of the elderly care team in 70 per cent of hospitals (Table 6.3). The degree of integration of the social worker in the hospital elderly care team was found to be important in another study, as follows. The quality of social work practice was rated positively by other health professionals where social workers identified with the hospital ethos, were accessible and worked regularly on the ward (Davies 1995). On the above measures, most teams in our study had managed to achieve collaborative working relationships, although nearly one-third of hospital elderly care teams could not be characterised as tightly integrated.

## Assessment processes

Are better care assessment processes associated with better care assessment? A composite measure of 'better assessment' was constructed by combining positive scores on two factors – better quality assessment and better patient outcomes. Cross-tabulations were run for 'better assessment' against other measures, although the numbers were not large enough for statistical analysis. The results for the 36 teams with 'better assessment' are shown in Table 6.4.

Teams that had 'better assessment' were more likely (70 per cent of teams) to be 'multidisciplinary' in assessing patients with multiple needs (five-plus staff assess nursing home patients, and

**Table 6.4** 'Better assessment' teams

| *Other factors* | *% (N = 36)* |
|---|---|
| 'Multidisciplinary' | 70% |
| 'Formal' | 56% |
| 'Teamwork' | 47% |
| 'Coordination' | 36% |

five-plus staff assess complex community care patients). This is consistent with the frequently expressed view that multidisciplinary assessment is 'best practice' (see for example, NHS Health Advisory Service 1997). Teams with 'better assessment' were also more likely to be more 'formal' (written health eligibility criteria, and written social services eligibility criteria, and hospital discharge protocols) as recommended in hospital discharge guidelines (Department of Health 1994). The 'teamwork' dimension (all cases discussed in staff meetings, and weekly ward meetings, and better staff relations) was a factor in only half these 'better assessment' teams. A composite measure of the 'coordination' dimension (screening for referral and formal assessment coordination) was not associated with 'better assessment'. Contrary to some research on teamwork (for example, Øvretveit et al 1997), the formal coordination of work within the team did not emerge as an important factor.

## Summary

Most social workers in the 54 hospital elderly care teams (nearly 90 per cent) thought that care assessment was now done better with clearer goals and procedures. Nearly 70 per cent thought that patients were getting better post-hospital services, at least 'high risk' patients, but were concerned that low dependency patients received little or no help. Over half thought that working relations with other staff were better. But nearly 40 per cent thought that their working relations with clients and families were worse, which they attributed to having to explain why social services could not help. Nearly 80 per cent said that case assessment took more time and nearly 60 per cent reported less job satisfaction. In summary, social workers said that they were doing better but feeling worse.

Working together was not easy, since hospital elderly care teams contain staff from different professions and employers and with different priorities. The teams that reported better assessment (better quality assessment and better service outcomes for clients) were more likely to follow formal procedures (written health and social services eligibility criteria and hospital discharge protocols), and to undertake multidisciplinary assessment with patients with multiple needs (by five or more staff). This suggests that multidisciplinary assessment and formal procedures are 'best practice'.

## *Part III*

# Patients and Services

7

# Patient Profiles

## Introduction

The policy intention of care assessment is that the services that people receive should be determined by their needs, rather than by the supply of available services, or by the professional background of the assessor. All three factors, however, may influence service allocation decisions.

### Needs-led services

The 1990 NHS and Community Care Act set out the fundamental community care concept that assessment should be 'needs-led'; that is, decisions about services should follow an assessment of a person's needs (Social Services Inspectorate 1991; Department of Health 1993). The normative assumption is that professionals identify the most 'needy' people and allocate the services most appropriate to those needs. It follows that patients with similar needs should receive similar post-discharge care services. Uniformity across geographic areas has never been a feature of UK social care provision, however, and policies have emphasised responsiveness to 'local needs'.

The main characteristics associated with entry to institutional care include old age, high dependency, and lack of a family carer. Most residents of UK residential and nursing homes are aged 75 years plus (40 per cent are aged 85 plus); the majority are women (since women live longer than men); most have multiple disabilities; most have no partner at home to care for them; and many are transferred directly from hospital to institutional care (Laing & Buisson 1997: 81). A national survey of all residents in Australian hostels and nursing homes identified the following characteristics. Most people were very old (two-thirds were aged 80 plus); most had high levels of functional dependency (95 per cent of nursing home residents required help with mobility and transfers); and they were less likely than community services users to have a family carer (Australian Institute of Health and Welfare 1997).

Predictors to the use of community services are less clear. There is little systematic research on the characteristics of community services users in the UK. There is some information on age: for example, the oldest client in nearly one-third of households receiving home help and home care in England in 1996 was 85 years plus (Department of Health 1997c). A national survey of Australian community service users found no old age-related trend and few clear predictors (Australian Institute of Health and Welfare 1997). Living alone was a more consistent predictor than functional status to the use of formal services in a USA longitudinal study of frail elders (Tennstedt et al 1990). Gender and class also have been found to affect the likelihood of receiving community services (Arber et al 1987).

## Service-led services

The intention of community care policy is to separate the consideration of needs from the type of services that are available. Assessment is meant to precede a service decision. This concept of a 'needs-led' rather than 'services-led' assessment has proved difficult to put into practice. First, 'need' is extremely difficult to separate from professional and organisational perspectives (Social Services Inspectorate 1991; Nolan & Caldock 1996; Futter & Penhale 1996). Second, need is a contested concept as the definition depends upon who defines the need (Bradshaw 1972). Third, severely limited resources have greatly constrained service choices in UK community care: 'The ideal might have been a "needs-led" service; the reality was undoubtedly a "service-led" service' (Allen et al 1992: 324).

## Professional-led services

Assessment of need may also be influenced by the professional background of the assessor. Perceptions of the best treatment decision vary between health professionals; for example, doctors and nurses differ in their views on whether to resuscitate a very old and terminally ill patient with dementia (Alemyehu et al 1991; Lever et al 1992). Perceptions of need also differ between professionals. One study asked assessment staff in community care projects to watch a video of an assessment interview and then complete a questionnaire: occupational therapists were far more likely to identify need for aids and equipment, while nurses identified need relating to illness (Petch 1996). Other studies have found that social workers believe that they are less likely than doctors and nurses to recommend institutional care (Moxley 1989; Healy 1994).

# Three elderly care teams

This study selected three elderly care teams in order to compare different team models in terms of service outcomes for patients. The intention was to keep other factors as constant as possible: similar patients, adequate post-hospital resources, formal assessment procedures, and staff perceptions of 'good' teamwork. This chapter summarises the three elderly care teams and their environment and describes the patient sample (N = 456). This overview sets the context for the analysis of referrals and services in the next chapter. The different staffing patterns in coordinating care assessment in the three elderly care teams are summarised as follows (see box overleaf):

- Team A made the nurse the main link;
- Team B gave the occupational therapist the lead role;
- Team C gave the social worker the lead role.

## Three Hospital Teams

### Team A

The elderly care unit had three wards (84 beds) with a mix of acute and short-stay rehabilitation beds. The multidisciplinary team comprised four consultants (including two geriatricians), the nurses included a nurse manager, two social workers plus the home care organiser (two whole time equivalents), a physiotherapist, and three occupational therapists (about two WTE). Separate working procedures made for a weaker team ethos than the other two teams.

Care assessment procedures were conducted separately, with the nurse being the main link. The named nurse screened and referred, completed a discharge form noting decisions made at the ward meeting, referred to community health services, and reactivated social services received by people prior to admission. The nurse previously had requested basic or 'simple' services from the area SSD office but this was now done by hospital social services.

Formal procedures and standard forms were used. The hospital discharge protocol set out who was to undertake which tasks and by when. Referrals were made on a standard form, and staff completed separate assessment forms. A consultant chaired the weekly ward meeting, attended by most staff. The social worker also attended one consultant's ward rounds. The nurse filled out the discharge form noting the services arranged.

The social services hospital team separated assessment and purchasing tasks. Simple assessments were done by the home care manager, and complex (mainly residential and nursing home) assessments by a social worker; staff ordered in-house SSD services; the team leader authorised other services up to a cost limit and other cases went to a SSD panel; and the home care manager or assistants arranged services. Case conferences were sometimes called to discuss complex cases. The hospital social services team followed patients and purchased services for four weeks after discharge.

The elderly care unit had access to a good supply of post-hospital health care services. The nearby community Trust had an 88 bed rehabilitation hospital and there were also two GP-run hospitals. There were no long-stay NHS beds. This local authority had the lowest per capita 75-plus social services expenditure for its population aged 75 years and over.

## Team B

The elderly care unit had three wards used for pre-discharge rehabilitation, stroke cases and general care. The multidisciplinary team displayed a moderate team ethos. Occupational therapists played a lead role in assessing people for discharge home, and pre-discharge home visits were a high priority. The multidisciplinary staff included two consultant geriatricians, ward nursing staff and a nurse manager, one and a half social work equivalents assigned to the three wards, two physiotherapists, two occupational therapists, and a nurse equipment manager.

Formal procedures and standard forms were used. The named nurse screened and referred using a standard form. The hospital social services team took new or urgent referrals, and the nurse referred current clients to their SSD area care manager. Weekly meetings for each ward were held post-ward round, chaired by a consultant, everyone attended and most cases were reviewed. Staff (except for social services) made notes on a joint assessment form. Separate more informal care assessment meetings were also held without the medical staff.

The social services hospital team separated assessment and purchasing tasks. Simple assessments (including the Aftercare scheme) were done by a care coordinator, and complex assessments by the senior care coordinator (social worker). The team leader authorised all domiciliary services up to a cost limit; expensive case recommendations (including all residential and nursing home placements) went to a SSD panel; a care coordinator or assistant arranged the purchase of services.

This team engaged in some task sharing. A nurse organised equipment for discharge; occupational therapists used to manage the pre-discharge ward now managed by nursing; nurses sometimes assessed activities of daily living on behalf of the occupational therapists; the social services care coordinator and occupational therapist did joint home visits, and the occupational therapist wrote up the joint care plan.

This team used a joint aftercare post-discharge scheme, managed by a nurse, whereby social services provided up to four weeks of care for a ceiling budget of £70 per week. NHS long stay beds were in the process of being closed with about 20 left. This local authority had the highest per capita 70+ annual expenditure, provided the most home care for very old clients, but was the socio-economically most deprived local authority area of the three.

## Team C

The elderly care unit had 40 beds in three connecting wards: rehabilitation, stroke, and palliative care. The multidisciplinary team had a strong ethos since staff met frequently and assessed most patients. There were two consultants, ward nursing staff and a nurse unit manager, one social work care manager, one physiotherapist, one occupational therapist, and a liaison nurse for the whole hospital who linked with community nursing and handled 'difficult' (delayed) discharges, especially to nursing homes.

Referral and assessment procedures were formal and standardised. The 'named nurse' screened and referred on a standard form via the hospital computer. A 'key worker' (nurse or therapist) assessed the 'health' aspects and the social worker the 'social' aspects. The social worker coordinated the various opinions. The occupational therapist did pre-discharge home visits with most patients going home. All staff (about eight) attended weekly ward rounds with each consultant as well as ward meetings which the consultant chaired. The 'named' or 'key worker' nurse entered assessment and discharge decisions from this meeting on a discharge summary form.

The generalist hospital social worker had an office on the unit and did all the care assessments (with no division into simple or complex cases), as well as means testing, costing, recommending, authorizing (up to the devolved case budget limit), and purchasing services. The hospital discharge protocol set one day to see the patient and another two days to complete the assessment. Hospital social services followed clients for up to four weeks.

The hospital had no NHS long stay beds left, but the region had the best supply of nursing home beds. This local authority was the middle of the three in terms of per capita social services expenditure on the older population, and was the most prosperous of the three geographic areas.

These teams worked in similar types of elderly care units, which had mixed wards in large acute care general hospitals, similar ratios of staff to patients, and practised formal care assessment procedures with standard forms (Table 7.1 and 7.2). The hospitals were in large towns, about 7 per cent of the local authority population was aged 75 years and over, and the local areas were around the middle range on an index of social and economic deprivation. Three measures of access to resources were used that showed some differences: Team A had access to the most post-hospital rehabili-

**Table 7.1** Elderly care teams

| *Factors* | *Team A* | *Team B* | *Team C* |
|---|---|---|---|
| Coordination | nurse | occupational therapist | social worker |
| Elderly care wards | 3 wards (84 beds) | 3 wards (54 beds) | 3 wards (40 beds) |
| Hospital department | General Medicine | General Medicine | General Medicine |
| Type of wards | mixed | mixed | mixed |
| Elderly care admissions | need or via wards | need or via wards | need or via wards |
| Core staff[1] | 5+ | 5+ | 5+ |
| Social worker: bed ratio | 1:42 | 1:54 | 1:40 |
| OT bed ratio | 1:42 | 1:36 | 1:40 |
| Unit/ward meetings | weekly | weekly | weekly |
| Social services post-hospital | 28 days | 14 days – community 28 days – institution | 28 days |
| SSD case budget ceiling pw (1996) | | | |
| nursing home | £313 | £320 | £347 |
| residential home | £235 | £220 | £247 |
| community services | £135 | £150 | £150 |

Notes: (1) Includes geriatrician, nurse, physiotherapist, occupational therapist, social worker and others.

tation services, Team B to the largest per capita social services expenditure, and Team C to the most nursing home places.

Factors relating to patient characteristics were selected from the research literature as likely to predict post-hospital services, subject to the availability of comparable data in the patient medical record. These included predisposing factors (such as patient age), enabling factors (such as patient having a carer), and needs (patient dependency and health status). Patients were selected into the study from all those discharged over nine months from January to September 1997, who were aged 75 plus, and had been admitted to hospital from private households.

**Table 7.2** Local environment

| *Factors* | *Team A* | *Team B* | *Team C* |
|---|---|---|---|
| Type of NHS Trust | acute | acute | acute & community |
| Local authority | County Council | Metro Borough Council | County Council |
| Local authority population aged 75+[1] | 7.6% (53,870) | 6.6% (20,620) | 7.9% (123,400) |
| Index of deprivation[2] | 179 | 143 | 246 |
| Post-hospital health care: | | | |
| NHS & SSD scheme Rehabilitation services | rehabilitation, day hospital, rehab hospital | aftercare, day hospital | district nursing, day hospital |
| Nursing home places | W Midlands | W Midlands | Home Counties |
| UK = 100[3] | 88 | 88 | 81 |
| Resi home places | W Midlands | W Midlands | Home Counties |
| UK = 100[3] | 95 | 95 | 121 |
| SSD net expenditure £ per capita 75+[1] | £749 | £1232 | £917 |
| Home care per 10,000 households[4] | | | |
| 75–84 years client | 584 | 1241 | 749 |
| 85+ client | 2428 | 4392 | 2810 |

*Sources:* (1) Chartered Institute of Public Finance and Accountancy CIPFA 1997;
(2) Dept of Environment 1994, 1=most deprived, 183=midpoint, 366=least deprived;
(3) Laing & Buisson 1997; Social Services Yearbook 1997; IHSM Health and Social Services Year Book 1996/97;
(4) Dept of Health *Community Care Statistics England 1996.*

## Patient characteristics: demographic

The characteristics of the sample of patients discharged from elderly care wards in the three hospitals are summarised below. (The few missing values in the frequency tables demonstrate that missing data did not prove to be a methodological problem.)

**Table 7.3** Patient characteristics: predisposing and enabling factors

| *Variables* | *Team A (N=179)* | *Team B (N=162)* | *Team C (N=114)* |
|---|---|---|---|
| Predisposing factors | | | |
| Age: | | | |
| 75–84 | 52% (94) | 58% (94) | 54% (62) |
| 85+ | 48% (85) | 42% (68) | 46% (52) |
| Sex: | | | |
| male | 32% (58) | 26% (43) | 35% (40) |
| female | 68% (121) | 74% (119) | 65% (74) |
| Lived alone: | | | |
| no | 43% (78) | 35% (57) | 42% (48) |
| yes | 55% (98) | 64% (104) | 55% (63) |
| missing values | 2% (3) | 1% (1) | 3% (3) |
| Enabling factors | | | |
| Family carer: | | | |
| yes | 68% (122) | 74% (119) | 69% (78) |
| no | 30% (53) | 24% (39) | 26% (30) |
| missing values | 2% (4) | 2% (4) | 5% (6) |

## Predisposing factors

Several factors were identified as likely to predispose people to needing assistance upon discharge from hospital. The patient sample results for these factors showed that these elderly care units treated similar groups of older people (Table 7.3).

*Age:* Of the total sample (selected on 75 years and over), over 40 per cent in each of the three hospitals were aged 85 years and over.

*Sex:* Over two-thirds of the sample in each hospital were women. This preponderance was expected, since 66 per cent of the total population aged 75 years-plus are female (Office for National Statistics 1998).

*Lives alone:* Nearly 60 per cent of the three groups of patients lived alone. This is consistent with the population profile in that over half of women aged 75-plus in private households live alone, rising to 70 per cent in the 85-plus age group (OPCS 1996).

## Enabling factors

An important factor determining whether a dependent person can continue to manage at home is whether they have a family carer; absence is a predictor for nursing home care, but not necessarily for all community services, since services such as district nursing often depend upon family care (Twigg & Atkin 1994; Australian Institute of Health and Welfare 1997).

*Family carer:* About one-quarter of these patients had no family carer, or at least none recorded on the patient medical record (Table 7.3). It was not always clear from the patient medical record whether or not the family carer resided in the home except in conjunction with the 'living alone' category.

# Patient characteristics: dependency

The main available measure of need was functional dependency. No standard measure was used in all three hospitals, such as the Barthel Scale, but three items from the various measures used were common to each hospital (mobility, continence and confusion): the presence or absence of problems was recorded (although not necessarily the severity). The named nurse (or the occupational therapist or physiotherapist) filled out functional dependency categories prior to discharge. A personal dependency score was constructed for this study on the above three activities of daily living. A score of 3 indicates problems in three selected areas and a score of 0 indicates no problems: 3=high dependency, 2=medium dependency, 1=low dependency, 0= no problems.

Over 70–90 per cent of patients in the three hospitals had at least one area of functional dependency upon discharge (Table 7.4). The mean dependency score suggests low to medium

**Table 7.4** Patient characteristics: dependency

| *Variables* | *Team A (N=179)* | *Team B (N=162)* | *Team C (N=114)* |
|---|---|---|---|
| Dependency on discharge: | | | |
| Any dependency | 70% (124) | 91% (148) | 90% (102) |
| No dependency | 29% (52) | 9% (14) | 10% (12) |
| Missing values | 1% (3) | 0% (–) | 0% (–) |
| Number of dependency areas: | | | |
| None | 29% (52) | 8% (14) | 10% (12) |
| One | 44% (79) | 54% (87) | 44% (50) |
| Two+ | 25% (45) | 37% (61) | 46% (52) |
| Missing values | 2% (3) | 0% (–) | 0% (–) |
| Mean dependency score (0–3) (3 missing cases) | 0.98 | 1.5 | 1.6 |
| Dependency: mobility | | | |
| No problem | 37% (67) | 12% (19) | 15% (17) |
| Has problem | 61% (109) | 88% (143) | 85% (97) |
| Missing values | 2% (3) | 0% (–) | 0% (–) |
| Dependency: continence | | | |
| No problem | 81% (145) | 78% (126) | 62% (71) |
| Has problem | 17% (31) | 22% (36) | 38% (43) |
| Missing values | 2% (3) | 0% (–) | 0% (–) |
| Dependency: confusion problem | | | |
| No problem | 76% (136) | 74% (120) | 74% (84) |
| Has problem | 22% (40) | 26% (42) | 26% (30) |
| Missing values | 2% (3) | 0% (–) | 0% (–) |

dependency, with people on average needing assistance in at least one area. Problems with mobility were common for over 60 per cent of these hospital patients, while over 20 per cent had problems with continence and with confusion. Team A patients had the fewest dependency problems. A person's functional abilities may improve after discharge from hospital, but, upon discharge, 60 per cent of this sample of older hospital patients had mobility problems and so were more dependent than the general population of older people living in private households.

**Table 7.5** Patient characteristics: number of medical conditions

| *Variables Medical conditions on discharge* | *Team A (N=178)* | *Team B (N=163)* | *Team C (N=114)* |
|---|---|---|---|
| One/two conditions | 70% (126) | 50% (81) | 67% (76) |
| Three plus conditions | 29% (52) | 50% (81) | 33% (38) |
| Mean number | 2.0 | 2.5 | 2.1 |

For example, in the 1994 General Household Survey, 15 per cent of 80–84 year olds and 30 per cent of people aged 85 plus needed help with climbing stairs (Office for National Statistics 1998, Table 8.21).

## Patient characteristics: health factors

The health characteristics of patients in the three hospital elderly care units were examined in relation to number of medical conditions: primary diagnosis upon discharge, length of stay, and prior hospital admission.

### Number of medical conditions upon discharge

Table 7.5 shows the number of medical conditions listed upon discharge, which was taken from the copy of the consultant letter to the patient's GP lodged in the patient medical record. Over one-third of the total sample had three-plus medical conditions listed. Forty per cent of Team B patients had three or more medical conditions compared to 29 per cent from Team A.

### Medical diagnosis upon discharge

Table 7.6 shows the primary diagnosis upon discharge for these patients. This was entered on the discharge summary sheet in the patient medical record and in the consultant's letter to the GP.

**Table 7.6** Patient characteristics: primary diagnosis upon discharge

| *Diagnosis (ICD codes A00-Z99)* | *Team A (N=179)* | *Team B (N=163)* | *Team C (N=114)* | *England*[1] *(N=410,291)* |
|---|---|---|---|---|
| Circulatory/heart (100–199) | 35% (63) | 30% (49) | 27% (31) | 26.9% |
| Injury & poisoning[2] (S00–T99) | 15% (26) | 37% (60) | 35% (40) | 4.2% |
| Respiratory (J00–J99) | 11% (20) | 3% (5) | 3% (3) | 15.6% |
| Digestive system (K00–K93) | 6% (10) | 3% (4) | 7% (8) | 6.5% |
| Nervous system & sense organs (G00–G99) | 3% (5) | 4% (6) | 4% (5) | 3.8% |
| Mental disorder (F00–F99) | 5% (8) | 2% (3) | 8% (9) | 1.9% |
| Neoplasm (C00–D48) | 6% (5) | 0.6% (1) | 4% (4) | 4.5% |
| Genito-urinary (N00–N99) | 4% (7) | 0 | 3% (3) | 3.2% |
| Other (All other codes) | 19% (34) | 22% (35) | 10% (11) | 33.3% |

*Source:* (1) Dept of Health unpublished tables; Finished consultant episodes, number of discharges from the Geriatric Medicine speciality by primary diagnosis 1995/96.
*Notes:* (2) All fractures coded as injury in hospital audit cases.

About 30 per cent of the sample had circulatory and heart problems, with no difference between hospitals. The next highest category was injury and poisoning (which included hip fractures). The population rate of accidents rises in older age groups. Falls account for 72 per cent of accident injuries treated by hospitals among those aged 75 years and over (Department of Trade and Industry 1997, HASS data). Team A had a lower proportion of injury cases, as the orthopaedic wards were in another hospital and later transferred patients with hip fractures and hip replacements to a rehabilitation hospital.

**Table 7.7** Patient characteristics: total days in hospital

| *Number of days* | *Team A (N=179)* | *Team B (N=162)* | *Team C (N=114)* |
|---|---|---|---|
| 0–29 | 67% (119) | 13% (22) | 40% (45) |
| 30–59 | 25% (45) | 51% (82) | 47% (54) |
| 60+ | 8% (15) | 36% (58) | 13% (15) |
| Mean days (Standard deviation) | 27.9 (23.0) | 58.3 (33.6) | 37.2 (21.5) |

*Note:* Percentages and means calculated on valid cases; days in elderly care ward are included in total days in hospital

Table 7.6 compares the discharge diagnosis to finished consultant episodes upon discharge for Geriatric Medicine, for the age group aged 75 plus, for hospitals in England (Department of Health computer tables). This category covers geriatrician episodes across all hospital beds and, although the best available, is not an exact comparison. Diagnostic categories are similar to the study sample, except that more patients were coded as injury cases in our sample, mainly fractured neck of femur and hip replacements; also, fewer patients were coded as 'other'.

## Length of stay

Nearly 20 per cent of patients spent 60 days or more in hospital and 59 per cent had spent 30 or more days (Table 7.7). The mean number of days varied considerably, from 27.9 in Team A to 58.3 days in Team B, but with large standard deviations. Most of these days in hospital were in the elderly care wards but the mode of admission was often via other wards (Table 7.8). A small number of patients (10 per cent) spent 60 or more days in the elderly care wards. The mean number of days patients spent in elderly care wards was 25 days in Team A, rising to 36 days in Team B. The length of stay pattern across the three elderly care units was therefore very similar, except for slightly longer stays with Team B, which specialised in pre-discharge rehabilitation.

**Table 7.8** Patient characteristics: days in elderly care ward

| *Number of days* | *Team A (N=178)* | *Team B (N=151)* | *Team C (N=113)* |
|---|---|---|---|
| 0–29 | 72% (129) | 51% (77) | 61% (69) |
| 30–59 | 29% (35) | 34% (37) | 33% (37) |
| 60+ | 8% (14) | 15% (22) | 6% (7) |
| Mean days (Standard deviation) | 25.0 (22.0) | 35.9 (26.1) | 27.3 (17.5) |

*Note:* Percentages and means calculated on valid cases

This length of stay was higher than the NHS average but this sample of patients was a slightly older age group. Over the five years from 1989/90 to 1994/95, the average length of NHS hospital stay in the geriatric speciality fell by 45 per cent from 36 to 20 days (Audit Commission 1997: 41, citing NHS Hospital Activity Statistics).

### Prior hospital admissions

About one-third or more of these patients had been admitted in the previous year and a small number in the previous month (Table 7.9). About 20 per cent of people aged 75 years and over enter hospital as inpatients each year (Department of Health 1992).

## Summary

Patients aged 75 years and over, who had been admitted from their own homes, were selected into this case review upon discharge from three hospital elderly care units over a nine-month time period. This produced a sample (N = 456) of predominantly older widows. Over 40 per cent of people were aged 85 years, two-thirds were women, and 60 per cent lived alone. Most had been in hospital for over four weeks, been treated for multiple medical

**Table 7.9** Patient characteristics: previous hospital admissions.

| *Variables* | *Team A (N=178)* | *Team B (N=161)* | *Team C (N=112)* |
|---|---|---|---|
| Previous month | | | |
| Admission | 3% (6) | 9% (14) | 16% (18) |
| Previous year | | | |
| No admission | 68% (122) | 63% (102) | 58% (66) |
| Admission | 31% (56) | 36% (58) | 42% (46) |

*Note:* Percentages calculated on valid cases

conditions, and over 70 per cent had at least one area of functional dependency. Given this profile, it might be expected that a high proportion would need assistance upon discharge from hospital.

The patients discharged from these three elderly care units were demographically similar, but differed somewhat in levels of dependency and health factors. Team A patients were less dependent, had fewer medical conditions, and fewer had been treated/rehabilitated for injuries such as hip fractures. Team B patients had the most number of medical conditions and stayed longest in hospital. Team C patients were closest in profile to Team B. The next step was to analyse patient referrals and services using the eight main variables identified in this chapter (Table 7.10).

The sex of the patient was dropped from the multivariate analysis model since this factor did not prove to be a better predictor of service patterns than the two other predisposing factors: old age and living arrangements. Length of stay in hospital was dropped from the medical factors since it did not emerge as an indicator to other measures of patient morbidity: number of medical conditions, prior hospital admission and also dependency.

The differences between patients discharged by the three teams were controlled for in the multivariate analysis presented in the next chapter.

**Table 7.10** Predictive variables: patient case review

| *Variable* | *Description* |
|---|---|
| *Structural* | |
| Team | Teams A, B, C |
| *Predisposing factors* | |
| Old age | 85+ years |
| Living arrangements | Lives alone |
| *Enabling factors* | |
| Family carer | No family carer |
| Service use on admission | Current user |
| *Need* | |
| Dependency | Two+ conditions |
| *Medical factors* | |
| Number medical conditions on discharge | Three+ |
| Prior hospital admission | Previous 12 months |

# 8

# Patients: Referrals and Services

## Introduction

The research issue is whether vulnerable older patients were referred for a care assessment, and what factors predicted the services that they received after discharge from hospitals. Patient characteristics or 'needs' were measured in this study by predisposing factors (such as age), enabling factors (such as having a family carer), functional need (such as dependency), and by health factors (such as number of medical conditions). Frequency tables on referrals and service patterns are shown for each hospital. The factors that may influence these patterns were then analysed using odds ratios and multivariate analysis.

## Referrals

Patients in these three teams mostly were screened by a 'named nurse' and referrals to other staff were made on a standard form, as required in hospital protocols, a copy of which was lodged in the patient medical record. In addition, referrals made later by other staff were entered on a standard form. Further, the researchers checked the patient medical record for notes about other referrals.

What proportion of patients were referred for a care assessment? The geriatrics literature recommends that all patients in hospital elderly care units should receive a multidisciplinary

**Table 8.1** Referral of patients for care assessment while in elderly care ward

| *Variable* | *Team A (N=179)* | *Team B (N=162)* | *Team C (N=114)* |
|---|---|---|---|
| Mean referrals (0–8) | 2.4 | 3.2 | 3.5 |
| Any referrals | 93% (166) | 100% (162) | 99% (113) |
| Social Services | 73% (131) | 69% (112) | 94% (107) |
| Occupational therapist | 65% (116) | 94% (152) | 88% (100) |
| Physiotherapist | 65% (117) | 96% (155) | 92% (105) |
| Dietician | 9% (16) | 25% (41) | 27% (31) |
| Speech therapist | 8% (15) | 18% (29) | 15% (17) |
| Specialist nurse | 7% (13) | 14% (23) | 23% (26) |
| Other | 8% (15) | 5% (8) | 11% (12) |

assessment (Kane 1985; Brocklehurst et al 1992). Less than one-third of the elderly care teams in our telephone survey (N = 54) said that all their patients were assessed by social services staff, although all complex cases were said to be assessed in three-quarters of hospitals. It was difficult to predict, therefore, what proportion of patients in these three hospital units would be referred for a care assessment or to how many staff.

This patient case review (N = 456) found that virtually all patients of the three selected hospital teams were referred to at least one professional for a formal care assessment (Table 8.1). Further, most patients were referred to more than one professional, the mean number ranging from 2.4 to 3.5 referrals per patient. These teams clearly followed recommended 'best practice', in that virtually all these older patients (who were a vulnerable group, as shown in Chapter 7) were referred for a multidisciplinary assessment. The most frequent referrals were to occupational therapy, social services and physiotherapy.

## Referral to occupational therapists

Was the type of referral associated with the type of professional who 'led' or coordinated the care assessment process? Were more patients referred for occupational therapy by Team B, where an occupational therapist coordinated care assessment? Team B patients, with 94 per cent referred to occupational therapy, had more referrals than Team C and many more than Team A (Table 8.1). Team B also referred more patients to physiotherapists, dieticians and speech therapists.

Team A was used as the baseline for calculating the odds ratios for Team B and Team C. The crude odds ratios show that Team B patients (the occupational therapy coordinated team) were eight times more likely to be referred to occupational therapy than those in Team A, and Team C patients were nearly four times more likely to be referred than Team A, and the adjusted odds ratios, adjusting for six types of patient characteristics, did not change this pattern in any major way (Appendix A.1). Logistic regression analysis added in variables in descending order of confounding potential. The most significant variables were then selected for analysis. 'Two-plus dependency conditions' and 'three-plus medical conditions' did not, however, independently predict the likelihood of a referral for an occupational therapy assessment (Table 8.2).

**Table 8.2** Referrals to occupational therapist for assessment

| *Referral to OT* | *Odds ratio* | *95% confidence interval* | *z* | *p>z* |
|---|---|---|---|---|
| Team B v A | 8.0 | 3.9–16.6 | 5.60 | 0.00 |
| Team C v A | 3.7 | 1.9–7.1 | 3.90 | 0.00 |
| 2+ dependency | 1.0 | 0.6–1.7 | –0.09 | 0.93 |
| 3+ medical conditions | 0.9 | 0.5–1.5 | –0.40 | 0.67 |

Although Team A patients were the most dependent group, this was not sufficient to explain the much higher pattern of referrals. Team B patients remained eight times more likely to be referred to occupational therapists than Team A patients, and over three times more likely to be referred than Team C patients.

## Referral to social services

Were more patients referred for a social services assessment by Team C, where care assessment was coordinated by the social worker? In Team C, 94 per cent of patients were referred for a social services assessment compared to 73 per cent in Team A and 69 per cent in Team B (Table 8.1).

The crude odds ratios show that Team C patients (the social work coordinated team) were over five times more likely to be referred for a social services assessment than patients of Team A, but there is little difference between Team B and Team A (Appendix A.2). The adjusted odds ratios for the six variables changed the figures only slightly. Logistic regression was applied, controlling simultaneously for 'two-plus dependency conditions', 'lives alone', 'no family carer' and 'a hospital admission in the previous month'. The model was improved when 'lived alone' and 'two-plus dependency conditions' were included. Patients who lived alone were 2.8 times more likely to be referred for a social services assessment (Table 8.3).

**Table 8.3** Referrals to social services for assessment

| *Referral to OT* | *Odds ratio* | *95% confidence interval* | *z* | *p>z* |
|---|---|---|---|---|
| Team B v A | 0.6 | 0.4–1.1 | –1.7 | 0.09 |
| Team C v A | 6.0 | 2.4–15.2 | 3.8 | 0.00 |
| 2+ dependency | 0.5 | 0.3–0.8 | –2.6 | 0.01 |
| Lives alone | 2.8 | 1.7–4.6 | 4.2 | 0.00 |

These results show that where care assessment was coordinated by a social worker (Team C), patients were six times more likely to be referred for a social services assessment than Team A patients and also more likely than Team B patients. Living alone also independently predicted a referral to social services. Notably, this was one of the 'trigger' questions on the screening form upon admission to hospital.

## Referral to specialist nurses

Were more patients referred to a specialist nurse for a home nursing assessment where care assessment was linked by the ward nurse? Team A, the nurse linked team, made fewer referrals for specialist nurse assessments but also made fewer referrals to all health professionals (dieticians and speech therapists), and fewer to social services. Team A referred only 7 per cent of patients for a specialist nurse assessment, Team B referred 14 per cent, and Team C referred 23 per cent (Table 8.1).

Stated as odds ratios, patients in Team B were twice as likely as those in Team A (the nurse linked team) to be referred for a home nursing assessment, whereas patients in Team C were nearly four times as likely to be referred than Team A. These referrals were primarily to a community liaison nurse. Patients of Team A were less sick and less disabled than patients in the other two hospitals, but controlling for these patient characteristics made little difference to the odds ratios (Appendix A.3). Logistic regression analysis tested for 'three-plus medical conditions' and 'no family carer', which might be expected to indicate a need for home nursing, but neither was independently related to referral (Table 8.4).

The proposition that Team A (the nurse linked team) would make more nursing referrals was not borne out. Team C (the social work coordinated team) referred patients most frequently to the nursing service. It could be argued, however, that Team A nurses, who were active in care assessment, did not need to obtain other nursing opinions. Team A nurses compared to nurses in the other teams spent more time on care assessment (as shown in Chapter 4).

**Table 8.4** Referrals to nursing services for assessment

| *Referral to OT* | *Odds ratio* | *95% confidence interval* | *z* | *p>z* |
|---|---|---|---|---|
| Team B v A | 2.1 | 1.0–4.3 | 1.9 | 0.05 |
| Team C v A | 4.0 | 2.0–8.2 | 3.8 | 0.00 |
| No family carer | 1.4 | 0.8–2.5 | 1.1 | 0.28 |
| 3+ medical conditions | 1.0 | 0.6–1.8 | 0.01 | 1.00 |

**Table 8.5** Post-hospital services arranged by hospital

| *Variable* | *Team A (N=179)* | *Team B (N=162)* | *Team C (N=114)* |
|---|---|---|---|
| Any (institutional, nursing or social) services | 88% (157) | 98% (159) | 91% (104) |
| Community (health/social) services | 71% (127) | 80% (130) | 61% (69) |
| Institutional care | 17% (30) | 18% (29) | 31% (35) |
| Refused community service[1] | 12% (22) | 2% (3) | 14% (16) |
| Refused institutional placement[1] | 1% (2) | 4% (6) | 3% (3) |

*Note:* (1) Some refused one type of community service but accepted another type, or did actually receive a service when discharged home despite the initial objection.

## Services arranged upon discharge

Did the post-hospital health and social care services arranged for patients upon discharge vary between the three teams? The three hospitals had a standard discharge form with sections for recording the post-hospital services that staff said that they had arranged. The patients in this study generally were quite old, most had some area of dependency, and virtually all were referred for a multidisciplinary assessment. The expectation was that most, therefore, would have some form of post-hospital assistance arranged. This proved to be the case, since all hospitals recorded arranging post-hospital services for the great majority of these older patients (including patients who before admission to hospital had been receiving a service). Services were arranged for 88 to 98 per cent of patients. Of the small proportion who did not have services arranged, some had refused the offer (Table 8.5). It was notable, therefore, that these elderly care teams arranged post-hospital services for nine out of ten of their elderly patients.

Community-based services (health or social care), were arranged for 71 per cent of patients in Team A, 80 per cent in Team B, and 61 per cent in Team C (Table 8.5). Team C (social

**Table 8.6** Post-hospital community health services arranged by hospital

| *Variable* | *Team A (N=179)* | *Team B (N=162)* | *Team C (N=114)* |
|---|---|---|---|
| District nurse | 30% (53) | 39% (63) | 26% (30) |
| Other community nurse | 25% (45) | 28% (45) | 9% (10) |
| Day hospital | 6% (11) | 15% (25) | 3% (3) |
| Physiotherapy | 5% (8) | 6% (10) | 14% (16) |
| Other community health | 12% (21) | 4% (6) | 2% (2) |

work-coordinated) was notable in that, although this team made the most referrals to other staff and to social services, it did not follow that this led to these services being agreed and arranged.

## Whether services were received

One measure of team effectiveness is whether the hospital elderly care team arranged the post-hospital services that one would predict based upon the 'needs' of older patients. Another measure of effectiveness is whether patients actually received the service arranged by the hospital after discharge. These elderly care teams invested considerable time and effort in assessing patients and deciding upon the appropriate post-discharge services. Did this assessment result in the service being delivered; in other words, did this assessment 'stick'? Three types of service were followed to ascertain whether these arranged services were actually received during the month after discharge: district nursing, social services (home/personal care), and institutional care (residential/nursing home placement). District nursing and social services are examined below and institutional care in a later section.

### District nursing services received

Team B arranged district nursing for most patients (39 per cent), compared to Team A (30 per cent) and Team C (26 per cent) (Table

**Table 8.7** District nursing services received pre-admission and post-discharge

| *Variable* | *Team A (N=179)* | *Team B (N=162)* | *Team C (N=114)* |
|---|---|---|---|
| District nursing prior to hospital admit | 19% (34) | 21% (34) | 10% (12) |
| Hospital arranged district nursing (including prior clients) | 30% (53) | 39% (63) | 26% (30) |
| District nursing received after discharge | 30% (53) | 33% (53) | 39% (45) |
| Mean number of weekly visits | 6 | 3 | 4 |
| District nursing received for at least four weeks | 64% (N = 53) | 65% (N = 53) | 78% (N = 45) |

8.6). Similar proportions of Teams A and B patients were current clients of district nursing when admitted to hospital (19 per cent and 21 per cent respectively), compared to only 10 per cent of Team C patients.

District or other types of community nursing were the most common type of post-hospital community health services received after discharge from hospital. In addition, a small proportion attended a day hospital or received physiotherapy (Table 8.7).

Were the district nursing services arranged by the hospital received? District nursing has considerable discretion on whether to accept a home nursing referral. The hospital nurse usually does not prescribe the home nursing needed, although hospital and community nurses often consult on complex cases. The expectation was that the nurse-linked team would have the most referrals accepted (in other words, would make appropriate assessments). Team A patients did receive services as arranged from the hospital, which suggests that appropriate referrals were made. Team B arranged nursing for more patients than received the service (39 per cent compared to 33 per cent), whereas more Team C patients received nursing than were recorded in the hospital, with 39 per

**Table 8.8** Post-hospital social care services arranged by hospital

| *Variable* | *Team A (N=179)* | *Team B (N=162)* | *Team C (N=114)* |
|---|---|---|---|
| Home/personal care | 35% (63) | 57% (92) | 39% (44) |
| Aids/equipment/house adaptations | 23% (41) | 62% (101) | 34% (39) |
| Meals (delivered/club) | 19% (34) | 12% (19) | 8% (9) |
| Respite admission | 6% (11) | 1% (1) | 4% (4) |
| Other social care services | 11% (20) | 6% (10) | 7% (8) |

cent compared to 26 per cent (Table 8.7). Apparently there were other routes into district nursing in this area in addition to the hospital. Over one-third of patients discharged by these elderly care teams did receive district nursing.

Over 60 per cent of district nursing patients from each of the hospitals received visits for at least four weeks after discharge, rather than a one-off home visit. This suggests that these patients were quite ill or dependent. More Team C district nursing patients received services for at least four weeks.

## Social services received

Most patients going home with social care services had a package arranged in which home/personal care was the core service (Table 8.8). This was received by 46 per cent of Team B, 34 per cent of Team C patients, 21 per cent of Team A (Table 8.7). Of those who received home/personal care, 15 per cent of Team A were clients before admission to hospital, Team B had 25 per cent, and Team C had the largest proportion with 32 per cent.

Team C arranged home/personal care for very few new clients while in hospital compared to the other hospitals, who organised services for another 20–25 per cent of patients. This suggests a rationing policy, since this local authority, which in previous years had expanded its community care spending, had cut back its budget and had begun to contract out all domiciliary services to the independent sector.

**Table 8.9** Social services (home/personal care) pre-admission and post-discharge

| *Variable* | *Team A (N=179)* | *Team B (N=162)* | *Team C (N=114)* |
|---|---|---|---|
| SSD client at hospital admission | 15% (26) | 25% (41) | 33% (37) |
| Referred to SSD for assessment | 73% (131) | 69% (112) | 94% (107) |
| SSD refused whilst in hospital | 12% (22) | 3% (4) | 14% (16) |
| Hospital arranged SSD home/personal care | 35% (63) | 57% (92) | 39% (44) |
| SSD home/personal care received* | 22% (38) | 46% (75) | 34% (38) |
| Social services received for at least four weeks | 84% (38) | 95% (75) | 89% (38) |
| Number of weekly mean hours | 16 | 31 | 33 |
| No change in services over four weeks | 81% (38) | 83% (75) | 76% (38) |

*Note:* * Percentages calculated on valid cases. Five case records missing from Team A post-hospital SSD sample.

Were the services arranged in hospital delivered? Since hospital social services authorised or 'purchased' post-discharge services, the expectation was that these services would be received. Did social care assessments done in hospital 'stick'? Fewer patients received home/personal care than were recorded as arranged in hospital. Team A organised for 35 per cent of discharges to receive home/personal care, but only 22 per cent did so; Team B arranged for 57 per cent, but only 46 per cent did so; while Team C showed the smallest discrepancy with 34 per cent receiving home/personal care.

Patients lived in the local authority area, so the discrepancy is not explained by services being provided elsewhere, and few older people moved house or died in the month after discharge. Several interpretations are possible. The ward nurse may have been overly optimistic in believing that services were arranged. Second, some people may have been found not to need home/personal care after they went home. This raises the question of whether assessments conducted in hospital can accurately assess people's need for assistance when they go home. The care plan for those who received the service was seldom altered after discharge, showing that the purchase or provision arrangement held. The SSD records were checked to ascertain whether the service package was changed over the course of the four post-hospital weeks from the initial amount arranged. Over three-quarters of clients did not have their hours of care altered and there was no consistent trend with the changes.

Over 80 per cent of home/personal care users in the three areas received services for at least four weeks. Few were allocated short-term services, therefore, which fits their higher dependency profile. Social service clients tended to get post-hospital assistance for longer than home nursing patients. The average social services hours per client over the four weeks differed markedly, with 30 hours for both Team B and C patients and only 16 hours in Team A.

## Predictors to post-hospital services

What factors predicted the receipt of post-hospital services? The main focus of the analysis was whether services were predicted by the type of hospital team or by the characteristics of the patients.

### Occupational therapy services arranged

Did the occupational therapy coordinated team (Team B) arrange more aids and equipment? Since it was not possible to check whether these services were delivered (as equipment was obtained from several providers), the analysis was applied to arranged (not received) services. Occupational therapists make an holistic assessment of patient needs and recommend various services –

**Table 8.10** Occupational therapy services arranged

| *Referral to OT* | *Odds ratio* | *95% confidence interval* | *z* | *p>z* |
|---|---|---|---|---|
| Team B v A | 5.5 | 3.4–8.9 | 6.9 | 0.00 |
| Team C v A | 1.8 | 1.1–3.0 | 2.2 | 0.03 |
| 2+ dependency | 1.3 | 0.8–1.0 | 1.1 | 0.27 |
| 3+ medical conditions | 1.1 | 0.8–1.7 | 0.6 | 0.52 |

but have primary responsibility for aids, equipment and house adaptations. Team B patients were five times more likely to have aids and equipment arranged than Team A, while Team C was nearly twice as likely to arrange services than Team A (Appendix A.4). Logistic regression controlled for 'two-plus dependency conditions' and 'three-plus medical conditions' simultaneously, but neither had any independent association (Table 8.10). Patient characteristics therefore had little effect. These results confirm the hypothesis that an occupational therapy coordinated process leads to more occupational therapy services arranged for patients upon discharge.

## District nursing

Did the team type or the characteristics of the patient account for the likelihood of receiving district nursing? The adjusted odds ratios, controlling for individual characteristics, show very little change from the crude ratios (Appendix A.5). Logistic regression controlled simultaneously for the following characteristics: 'two-plus dependency conditions', 'three-plus medical conditions', 'lives alone' and 'no family carer' (Table 8.11). Despite some minor adjustment, the team had little effect upon who received district nursing. Two-plus dependencies was the best predictor to receiving post-hospital nursing. Team A patients (the nurse-linked model) were not more likely, therefore, than patients from Team B and C to have district nursing arranged. This suggests that the characteristics of the patients, not the staff, predict whether patients will receive post-hospital community nursing.

**Table 8.11** Home nursing services received post-hospital

| *Referral to OT* | *Odds ratio* | *95% confidence interval* | *z* | *p>z* |
|---|---|---|---|---|
| Team B v A | 1.2 | 0.7–1.9 | 0.7 | 0.49 |
| Team C v A | 1.7 | 1.0–2.8 | 1.9 | 0.05 |
| Lives alone | 0.6 | 0.4–1.0 | –1.9 | 0.06 |
| No family carer | 1.3 | 0.8–2.1 | 1.0 | 0.31 |
| 2+ dependency | 1.8 | 1.1–2.8 | 2.5 | 0.01 |
| 3+ medical conditions | 1.4 | 0.9–2.1 | 1.5 | 0.14 |

## Social services

Did more Team C patients (social work coordinated team) receive home/personal care controlling for patient characteristics? Team B patients (the occupational therapy team) were most likely to receive post-hospital social services, followed by Team A patients. Patient characteristics did not affect this pattern in any major way (Appendix A.6). Logistic regression analysis (Table 8.12) controlled for the following characteristics independently: 'lived alone', 'no family carer', and 'two plus dependency conditions'. Patients discharged by Team B were nearly three times more likely to receive home/personal care than Team A, and those discharged by Team C were nearly twice as likely to receive services than those discharged by Team A. Living alone also independently predicted post-hospital social services.

## Discharge to institutional care

Was the likelihood of a patient being discharged to institutional care influenced by the team type or by patient needs? Admissions to a residential or nursing home were checked in the SSD records. Residential and nursing homes were not coded separately in this study, since the two were not always distinguished in the patient medical record and some homes have dual registration. All patients recorded in the hospital patient medical record as being transferred to institutional care were admitted. The few extra

**Table 8.12** Social services received post-hospital

| *Referral to OT* | *Odds ratio* | *95% confidence interval* | *z* | *p>z* |
|---|---|---|---|---|
| Team B v A | 2.9 | 1.8–4.7 | 4.2 | 0.00 |
| Team C v A | 1.8 | 1.1–3.2 | 2.2 | 0.03 |
| Lives alone | 1.7 | 1.1–2.7 | 2.2 | 0.03 |
| No family carer | 1.1 | 0.7–1.8 | 0.4 | 0.70 |
| 2+ dependency | 1.0 | 0.6–1.5 | –0.2 | 0.84 |

admissions were patients admitted for respite care who were still resident after one month and who were counted in this study as institutional care residents. Twenty per cent of Team A patients entered a residential or nursing home, 18 per cent of Team B and 34 per cent of Team C (Table 8.13).

When differences in patient characteristics were controlled, the adjusted odds ratios indicate little difference between teams in the likelihood of being discharged to institutional care (Appendix A.7). Controlling for the effect of these variables simultaneously did not change the adjusted odds ratios. Logistic regression analysis tested for 'old age', 'lived alone', 'no family carer', and 'two-plus dependency conditions', which all (except for dependency) independently increased the likelihood of entry to institutional care (see Table 8.14). Patient characteristics, therefore, were the best predictors to institutional care.

**Table 8.13** Institutional care received in month after discharge

| *Variable* | *Team A (N=179)* | *Team B (N=162)* | *Team C (N=114)* |
|---|---|---|---|
| Hospital arranged resi/ nursing home | 17% (30) | 18% (29) | 31% (35) |
| Resi/nursing home received after discharge | 20% (35) | 18% (29) | 34% (39) |

**Table 8.14** Institutional care received post-hospital

| *Referral to OT* | *Odds ratio* | *95% confidence interval* | *z* | *p>z* |
|---|---|---|---|---|
| Team B v A | 0.7 | 0.4–1.2 | –1.2 | 0.21 |
| Team C v A | 1.5 | 0.8–2.8 | 1.4 | 0.17 |
| Lives alone | 1.7 | 1.0–3.1 | 1.9 | 0.06 |
| No family carer | 1.6 | 0.9–2.8 | 1.6 | 0.12 |
| 2+ dependency | 0.2 | 0.1–0.3 | –6.9 | 0.00 |
| Old age | 1.7 | 1.0–2.8 | 2.1 | 0.04 |

## Delayed discharge

The precise definition of a 'delayed discharge' is problematic (Audit Commission 1997: 20). For example, a patient might be recorded as 'medically fit for discharge' in the sense of having completed acute care treatment but be waiting for hospital test results or be undergoing a rehabilitation programme. A few days delay is costly to a hospital since the average unit cost for one day in hospital was £114 (Netten & Dennett 1996: 71). Delayed discharge is said to be more common with older patients. In a survey of hospital patients aged 75 years and over, 20 per cent had remained in hospital beyond the medical discharge date (National Association of Health Authorities and Trusts 1995). In two hospitals cited by the Audit Commission (N=594 patients), the number of days of 'inappropriate length of stay' was nearly three times higher for those aged 75 plus than for those aged less than 65 years. The largest group were 'convalescing', followed by those receiving remedial treatment, or waiting for medical test results (Audit Commission 1997: 44). In another hospital, the proportion of delayed cases said to be waiting for social services department action dropped from 65 to 12 per cent after clear definitions of responsibility and procedures were agreed (Audit Commission 1997: 20). The length of hospitalisation of frail older people is usually linked to biomedical factors, but one study found that having a co-resident carer was associated with shorter hospitalisation (Skinner et al 1994).

**Table 8.15** Three-plus days delayed discharge

| *Variable* | *Team A (N=179)* | *Team B (N=162)* | *Team C (N=114)* |
|---|---|---|---|
| Three-plus days delay | 44% (78) | 14% (23) | 18% (21) |
| Any delay recorded | 75% (134) | 21% (35) | 23% (26) |

In this patient case review, the Team A hospital recorded the 'date of decision to discharge' on a standard discharge form. This was the date the consultant regarded the patient as being 'medically fit' for discharge. The other two hospitals did not have a 'date fit for discharge' category on a standard form in the patient medical record, but the nurse ward managers said that any significant delay was recorded – no 'date medically fit for discharge' note meant no delay. In all three hospitals, however, a delay of a day or so was not necessarily regarded by ward staff as 'bed blocking'.

Team A had 75 per cent of patients recorded as staying beyond the expected date of discharge, which seemed a very large proportion (Table 8.15), while the other two hospitals each had about 20 per cent of patients with recorded delays. Only 35 patients across the three elderly care units remained for seven days or more, but of these, eight patients remained for two weeks or more past the discharge date. A small number of patients, therefore, account for a large number of days of 'inappropriate length of stay'.

The proportions of delayed discharge patients in Teams B and C were similar to the 20 per cent that might be expected (National Association of Health Authorities and Trusts 1995). The high Team A proportion may be inflated by the recording effect, while Team B and C patient delays may be an underestimate, since patients who stayed a day or so longer are not seen as 'bed blocking'. The following procedure took account of these factors.

Recording ambiguities in the patient medical record were taken into account by selecting only patients with a recorded delay of three-plus days. Team A still had the largest proportion with 44 per cent, Team B had 14 per cent and Team C had 18 per cent. The characteristics of these 'delayed discharge' patients are examined in the following analysis.

**Table 8.16** Characteristics of delayed discharge patients and non-delayed patients

| | *Delayed (N=122) % (number)* | *Non-delayed (N=332) % (number)* |
|---|---|---|
| Aged 85 plus | 52 (64) | 42 (141) |
| Live alone* | 67 (82) | 56 (183) |
| No family carer* | 41 (49) | 22 (73) |
| Two plus dependency | 62 (76) | 66 (218) |
| Three plus medical conditions | 32 (39) | 40 (132) |
| Sixty plus days in hospital | 16 (19) | 21 (70) |
| Admission in previous year | 31 (38) | 37 (122) |
| Residential/nursing home entry* | 34 (42) | 18 (61) |
| District nurse post-discharge*[1] | 45 (30) | 35 (115) |
| Social services post-discharge[1] | 33 (39) | 34 (112) |

*Note:* * Differences between groups significant at P=0.05 or greater.
(1) Excluding residential/nursing home cases.

The delayed discharge patients (across the three hospitals) were more likely than the non-delayed patients to live alone, to have no family carer, and to enter institutional care, or receive home nursing for those who returned home (Table 8.16). Since some of these factors are probably related, confounding effects were investigated using multivariate analysis.

Patients in Team A were more likely than those in Team B or C to be delayed, controlling for patient characteristics (Appendix A.8). The adjusted odds ratio showed that controlling for 'recent hospital admission' had a marginal effect upon the relationship between hospital team and delayed discharge. Logistic regression analysis tested for the six variables, and having 'no family carer' was independently related to hospital delay. The question of whether patients were delayed because they were waiting for services was also tested. Receiving either district nursing or social services was not associated with delay (Table 8.17, 8.18), but being discharged to institutional care was independently associated with a delayed discharge (Table 8.19).

**Table 8.17** Delayed discharge in three hospitals, controlling for patient characteristics and post-hospital social services

| *Referral to OT* | *Odds ratio* | *95% confidence interval* | *z* | *p>z* |
|---|---|---|---|---|
| Team B v A | 0.18 | 0.1–0.3 | –5.8 | 0.00 |
| Team C v A | 0.30 | 0.1–0.5 | –4.5 | 0.00 |
| No family carer | 2.40 | 1.5–3.9 | 3.6 | 0.00 |
| 2+ dependency | 0.60 | 0.4–1.0 | –1.9 | 0.06 |
| Social services received | 1.30 | 0.8–2.2 | 1.1 | 0.29 |

**Table 8.18** Delayed discharge in three hospitals, controlling for patient characteristics and post-hospital district nursing

| *Referral to OT* | *Odds ratio* | *95% confidence interval* | *z* | *p>z* |
|---|---|---|---|---|
| Team B v A | 0.2 | 0.1–0.4 | –5.7 | 0.00 |
| Team C v A | 0.3 | 0.1–0.5 | –4.3 | 0.00 |
| No family carer | 2.3 | 1.4–3.6 | 3.4 | 0.00 |
| 2+ dependency | 0.7 | 0.4–1.1 | –1.7 | 0.09 |
| District nursing received | 0.9 | 0.5–1.4 | –0.5 | 0.58 |

**Table 8.19** Delayed discharge in three hospitals, controlling for patient characteristics and discharge to institutional care

| *Referral to OT* | *Odds ratio* | *95% confidence interval* | *z* | *p>z* |
|---|---|---|---|---|
| Team B v A | 0.2 | 0.1–0.4 | –5.5 | 0.00 |
| Team C v A | 0.2 | 0.1–0.4 | –4.6 | 0.00 |
| No family carer | 2.1 | 1.3–3.4 | 3.0 | 0.00 |
| Institutional care | 2.6 | 1.6–4.4 | 3.6 | 0.00 |

## Unplanned outcomes

Older people are said to have a high number of hospital re-admissions. Harding (1997: 6) cites frequent emergency re-admissions to hospital of older people within 28 days of discharge, suggesting that people are either discharged too early or are given

**Table 8.20** Unplanned outcomes in month after hospital discharge

| *Variable* | *Team A (N=179)* | *Team B (N=162)* | *Team C (N=114)* |
|---|---|---|---|
| Hospital readmit | 7% (12) | 7% (12) | 5% (6) |
| Died | 2% (4) | 1% (2) | 4% (4) |
| Moved | 0% (0) | 0% (0) | 4% (4) |

inadequate follow-up care once they get home. There were few hospital readmissions during the four-week follow-up period in this study and few differences between the teams. Both Team A and B readmitted 7 per cent of their patients, and Team C readmitted 5 per cent (Table 8.20). As shown earlier, admissions in the month previous to this hospital admission were 3 per cent in Team A, 9 per cent in Team B and 16 per cent in Team C. These three elderly care teams, which were selected as examples of 'good practice', did not therefore operate a 'revolving door' policy of premature discharge resulting in a readmission. However, a one in ten readmission rate is not insignificant.

There was a small proportion of other unplanned outcomes in the four weeks after hospital discharge, such as patients dying or moving out of the area, but these numbers were too small for statistical analysis.

## Summary

Virtually all patients of these three elderly care teams were referred to at least one professional for a formal care assessment. Referrals to professional staff (occupational therapist, social worker and specialist nurse) generally were predicted by the team model (professional-led assessment) not by patient characteristics (needs-led assessment). Team A (the nurse-linked team) made the fewest referrals per patient although these nurses spent considerable time themselves on assessment. Team B (the occupational therapy coordinated team) were most likely to refer for an occupational therapy assessment. Team C (social work coordinated) referred patients to more staff (an average of 3.5 referrals per patient) and was most likely to refer patients for a social services assessment.

These hospital teams arranged community or residential services for 90 per cent or more of their patients (including current service users). Hospital staff commit considerable time and effort to assessing patients and arranging post-hospital services. This does not always result in patients receiving the services. Most older patients received post-hospital district nursing and institutional care as arranged, but a small proportion did not receive help at home from social services.

What factors predicted the post-hospital services that people received? Team B patients (the occupational therapy coordinated team) were most likely, controlling for patient characteristics, to have aids and equipment arranged. For district nursing, received by about one-third of patients after discharge, patient characteristics (high dependency and multiple medical conditions) were more important factors than the team model. The receipt of home/personal care was not explained by patient characteristics or by the team model. The team with the largest amount of social services use (by 46 per cent of patients) had the largest per capita social services budget.

About one-third of patients were discharged to a residential or nursing home. Entry to institutional care was explained by patient characteristics (old age, living alone, no family carer), suggesting a consensus on the need for residential or nursing home care.

Delayed discharge was associated with having no family carer and being discharged to institutional care. Delay was more likely in Team A (the nurse-linked team), controlling for patient characteristics.

# 9

# Conclusions

## Introduction

A stay in hospital is often a turning point in the lives of dependent older people. Hospital elderly care teams must decide whether to assist older patients to return home with support or whether to arrange their entry to a residential or nursing home. The staff in hospital elderly care teams now work under greater pressure, with increasing numbers of people entering hospital from the growing 'old old' population. These staff come from different disciplines, have different employers and arguably have different priorities. The hospital staff focus upon discharge – the services that people need in order to leave hospital; while the social services staff focus upon care assessment – the services that people need after they leave hospital. Hospitals wish to discharge people expeditiously; health authorities wish to limit NHS continuing care costs; and social services wish to ration scarce social care to the most needy.

## Multidisciplinary assessment

Multidisciplinary assessment has long been promoted as 'best practice'. A positive finding from this study, therefore, is that multidisciplinary assessment is common practice in hospital elderly care teams. What this means in terms of who does what, and how, was less easy to analyse. Care assessment is a complex task since it serves several purposes, means different things to different staff, is done in different ways, and takes varying amounts of time. For example, a multidisciplinary assessment might involve a five-minute discussion in a ward meeting or take 20 hours of staff time including completing functional dependency measures. Also, staff have different views on what constitutes an assessment; for example, ward nurses described the admission screening interview as assessment, while social services staff regarded it as a referral. Further, the involvement of social services staff in assessment was often in their role as purchasers of post-hospital care rather than as contributors to a multidisciplinary assessment.

*A key finding from this study was the considerable variation in care assessment across elderly care units – both in who conducts assessments, and how these are conducted.*

The survey of 54 hospital elderly care teams found that several staff assessed older patients with multiple needs for post-hospital care. Five or more staff assessed patients for a complex community care package in three-quarters of these teams (N = 54), and assessed patients for a residential or nursing home place in nearly 70 per cent of teams. This 'core' team was supplemented by another five people (although general practitioners were notable by their absence). The five core staff always involved where patients had multiple needs were, in order: the social worker, nurse, consultant, occupational therapist and physiotherapist. In the teams that practised multidisciplinary procedures (five-plus staff always assessed complex cases), the social worker rated care assessment as of a better standard (better quality and better service outcomes).

*Hospital elderly care units carry out multidisciplinary care assessment both as best practice and as common practice. In the teams that practised multidisciplinary procedures, staff rated their standard of care assessment as better.*

The claim from the survey of 54 hospitals teams, that multidisciplinary assessment was both best practice and common practice, was confirmed in the patient case review of people aged 75 years and over (N = 456) in elderly care units of three selected hospitals. The characteristics of the patients suggested that a formal care assessment was appropriate for this vulnerable population. Most were elderly widows (over 40 per cent were aged 85 years and over) who lived alone, had at least one area of functional dependency upon discharge from hospital, and multiple medical conditions. Virtually all patients were referred for a care assessment by two or more staff, the mean number of referrals being 2.4 in Team A, 3.2 in Team B and 3.5 in Team C. Further, over 90 per cent of these older patients had services arranged for them upon discharge from hospital (although some were clients of community agencies before entering hospital). About one-third received post-hospital district nursing, one-third received personal/home care, and 20 per cent entered institutional care (a residential or nursing home).

*The health and social services sectors were endeavouring to produce a 'seamless service' for dependent older patients of the three selected hospital elderly care units, since over 90 per cent had post-hospital assistance arranged.*

## Better assessment

Department of Health guidelines since the 1990 NHS & Community Care Act have required district health authorities and local authority social services departments to clarify their respective responsibilities for patients upon discharge from hospital, and to jointly agree upon criteria and procedures. The policy intention was to produce a 'seamless service': patients should not be discharged home without the needed assistance, nor experience a gap before community services took over from hospital care, nor wait in hospital while 'cost-shifting' disagreements were resolved.

## Better service outcomes

Nearly 70 per cent of social workers in these 54 teams said that patients were getting better post-hospital services since the new community care policies had been introduced from 1993 onwards. This was a surprisingly positive finding given the criticisms of post-hospital community care (for example, Audit Commission 1997). However, most respondents qualified this view by saying that while high dependency patients were getting better and more appropriate services, low dependency patients were getting little or no help. Notably, nearly 40 per cent of social workers said that their relations with patients and families were worse, since funding shortages meant that they were unable to offer help. Priority was given to people with multiple needs who required a complex package of care while people needing only single or short-term services were a low priority group. Recent government reports have also expressed concern about the erosion of preventive services (House of Commons 1996; Audit Commission 1997; NHS Health Advisory Service 1997). The main arguments are that a little help early on may prevent later deterioration, and that older people and their family carers are entitled to help in maintaining a decent quality of life. More research is needed to examine whether a little help earlier would enable older people to live independently in their own homes for longer. There is also the social rights argument that people are entitled to enjoy a good quality of life in old age.

*The majority of hospital elderly care teams thought that high dependency patients were getting better and more appropriate services. Small amounts of assistance to less needy people were no longer offered, however, although preventive help may produce better outcomes for older people as well as improving their quality of life.*

## Better assessment procedures

This survey of 54 hospital teams (carried out in July 1996) found that key guidelines on care assessment procedures for older hospital patients, set out in Department of Health documents, mostly had been implemented. Care assessment procedures in these 54 hospitals had improved in the following ways:

- procedures were more transparent, with published patient eligibility criteria and procedures;
- procedures were more formal, with designated assessment and discharge decisions points;
- procedures were more standardised, with forms and documentation.

Nearly 90 per cent of hospital social workers (N = 54) said that the standard of care assessment was better under the new guidelines. The teams where the social worker rated care assessment as better (better quality and better service outcomes) were associated with formal procedures (written eligibility criteria and discharge protocols). This positive finding confirms the value of Department of Health efforts to require clear agreements between sectors as well as formal assessment procedures.

*Clear agreements between health and social services on respective responsibilities for post-hospital care, and formalised work procedures, were associated with better ratings for care assessment. Official policies should continue to reinforce formal working relationships between the health and social services sectors.*

## Formal procedures

Formal procedures are important since hospital elderly care staff work in loose rather than tightly integrated teams: staff come from different disciplines, work across hospital wards, answer to different line managers and employers, and have different priorities. Over half of social services staff said that working relations with hospital staff were better now that responsibilities and procedures were clearer. Four key procedures are discussed below.

*Published criteria and protocols:* Most health authorities and social services departments in this study (N = 54 hospitals) had produced eligibility criteria for post-hospital care: about 80 per cent of health authorities had published their eligibility criteria, as had 90 per cent of social services departments. Nearly 80 per cent of these hospitals used discharge protocols that typically set out decision points, designated staff and time frames.

*Referrals for care assessment:* About half of hospitals designated a staff member (usually the ward nurse) to screen patients upon admission on their likely need for post-hospital assistance. Screening involved an early referral of patients in the interests of smoother discharge arrangements, although referrals were also made later in the hospital stay, by other staff, and in the ward meeting. Social services staff complained that they found it difficult to persuade hospital staff that 'best practice' (and the 1990 NHS and Community Care Act) required a service decision to follow, not precede, an assessment. The importance of multiple referral points is underlined by the finding, discussed later, that referrals in the patient case review (N = 456) are often predicted by the team staffing model, not the characteristics of the patient.

*Coordination:* Weekly ward meetings, usually chaired by the consultant, are a traditional forum for coordinating patient treatment activities. In two-thirds of hospitals, these were the main forum for staff from different disciplines to put their views, although a designated staff member also was responsible for coordinating the care assessment process. Coordination was important given the complexity of the process, with up to ten different staff involved where patients had multiple needs. The social worker was the designated coordinator in most hospitals, followed by the nurse. Which staff member took the coordination role affected referrals and services outcomes, as discussed later.

Hospital elderly care teams varied considerably in how care assessment tasks were allocated between staff. The complexity of the care assessment process requires coordination in relation to both staff (an accepted coordinator) and procedures (a shared assessment form, a care/discharge coordination meeting).

*Budgetary control:* Despite the expectation in the 1989 White Paper that care managers would manage budgets, financial constraints have brought more controls. Resource decisions had moved upwards to managers as budgets became tighter. Few social workers within the elderly care teams (N = 54) had the power to authorise a standard package of community services (only about 14 per cent) and virtually none could authorise residential or nursing home care. Most social services departments had case-level budget limits for community care packages and residential and nursing home places. One-fifth of social workers said that disputes over who should pay were endemic. These cost-shifting disputes were between health authority and social services managers, not team members, however, since managers, not care workers, controlled case-level budgets.

*Split responsibility for funding post-hospital social care combined with tighter budgetary control have made for extremely complex and lengthy procedures, over which hospital elderly care team members have little control. Ways to streamline these decisions should be found, such as joint funding for post-hospital care schemes.*

## Standard forms

Standard forms were increasingly used, but shared forms were rare across the professional and sector divide, since there was little consensus on common categories of information in relation to care assessment. The disadvantages of standard forms should also be noted, since 80 per cent of social workers said that care assessment took more time, although this was mainly due to the 'paper work' associated with the introduction of purchasing tasks.

*Interprofessional communication:* Standard forms had improved communication in care assessment. First, a screening form was used (in the ten hospitals visited) to refer patients upon admission for a care assessment. Second, in most hospitals social services staff now insisted upon a formal referral and no longer accepted 'coffee break' referrals. Third, a patient discharge form filled out by the ward nurse or ward manager was the nearest thing to a combined care plan in the ten hospitals visited.

Shared assessment forms were not used in any of these ten hospitals since the different professions used their own instruments. These forms showed considerable duplication in the information collected by nurses, occupational therapists and social workers. The nearest to a shared form was a joint assessment form lodged in the patient medical record in one hospital with summaries by the nurse and therapists but not by social services. The social services care plan in the ten hospitals visited was really a purchasing document lodged in social services department files but not in the patient medical record. The lack of a shared assessment form is a missed opportunity to integrate health and social aspects and to reduce duplication.

Many examples of inter-professional duplication emerged in this study, in relation to completing forms, but also in undertaking care assessment tasks. Some examples are as follows. The nurse screening interview with the patient elicits much similar information to an initial social services assessment. The social worker and the occupational therapist assessment duplicates information on some issues. Nurses, therapists and social workers collect much similar functional dependency information. Hospital-based staff and nursing home staff often duplicate assessments.

*Comparability:* The nursing profession tended to use comparable forms for assessment in the ten hospitals visited, such as Barthel Scales on functional dependency. In contrast, no comparable assessment instrument was evident across social service departments. Patient case audits increasingly are conducted in the health care sector in order to improve standards of care but are less common in the social services sector. But without a consensus on a national assessment protocol and without comparable data categories, it would be difficult to conduct a care assessment audit. For example, this study was constrained by the lack of comparable data. Any national equity policy on community care would require an audit on who gets what and why (Carpenter & Calnan 1997).

*A standard care assessment form should be sought in order to reduce duplication in multiple assessments by staff, and to monitor inequities in who gets what across local areas.*

## Service outcomes

The patient case review (N = 456) compared three selected hospital elderly care teams where different 'lead' staff coordinated the care assessment process: nurse, occupational therapist, and social worker. Three stages were examined: referrals for services, arranged services, and the receipt of services in the month after discharge. We found that virtually all older patients were referred for a formal care assessment and over 90 per cent had services arranged in the month after discharge. A main aim was to examine whether services were associated with the team staffing model or with patient characteristics.

*The great majority of older patients in these three hospital elderly care units received post-hospital health and social care services.*

### Nursing

Team A (the nurse-linked team) made the fewest referrals per patient, but did not make more referrals than would be expected (controlling for patient characteristics) for a specialist nurse assessment. Nurses in this team spent considerable time themselves on care assessment, and perhaps did not need to refer to a co-professional such as the liaison district nurse. The receipt of district nursing services by (one-third of) patients was predicted by the characteristics of the patients, not the team model. These tended to be high dependency patients. Several factors might explain this apparent consensus by nurses on the need for post-hospital nursing care. The health need for nursing may be straightforward to identify, and the nursing profession uses similar categories on nursing need, and similar assessment instruments (such as Barthel Scales). Patient access to district nursing also may be less budget driven than social care since the nursing service was less intensive (in terms of duration of visits and period of service). Patient characteristics, therefore, predicted both a referral for a nursing assessment and the receipt of district nursing services

*Patient characteristics predicted both referrals for a nurse asessment and access to post-hospital nursing services. This suggests a professional consensus among nurses on a patient's need for post-hospital nursing care.*

## Occupational therapy

Patients in Team B (the occupational therapy coordinated team) were eight times more likely than those in Team A to be referred for an occupational therapy assessment, controlling for patient characteristics. This elderly care unit emphasised pre-discharge rehabilitation. Team B patients were five times more likely (than Team A) to have occupational therapy services arranged for them upon discharge from hospital, controlling for patient characteristics. The professional (occupational therapist), not the characteristics of the patient, therefore, predicted both a referral for occupational therapy and the arrangement of occupational therapy services. Team B, however, worked in the SSD area with the highest per capita budget, which probably improved access to aids and equipment.

*Patients of occupational therapy coordinated care assessment were far more likely than those in other teams to be referred for an OT assessment, and to have aids and equipment arranged, controlling for patient characteristics. The greater availability of these services was likely to also be a factor.*

## Social services

Team C (social work coordinated) referred the most patients to more staff (an average of 3.5 referrals per patient) and referred the most patients for a social services assessment. The receipt of services in the month after discharge was checked with social services departments and about one-third of patients (N = 456) received personal/home care. Team B patients were more likely to receive post-hospital social services, however, than Team C (the social worker coordinated team). Team B also had the largest per capita social services budget, as noted above. Living alone was the best independent predictor to receipt of social services.

The picture for social services, therefore, was more complex than for other service types, for various reasons. The need for social care may be more difficult to assess, there was no common assessment instrument, there was less professional consensus on the need for social care, and there were considerable differences between local authorities in per capita social services funds. These results suggest that while referral for a social services care assessment was professional-led, the receipt of services was service-led, since the services that people received were rationed by the resources available.

*Patients of the social work coordinated assessment procedure received a more comprehensive multidisciplinary assessment but were not more likely to receive social services.*

## Institutional entry

About 20 per cent of these patients were discharged to institutional care (a residential or nursing home). The characteristics of these patients were the best predictors to entry to institutional care, not the team model. These people were more likely to have no family carer, to be very old, and to live alone. This suggests that there was a consensus across the three hospital teams on a person's need for institutional care. It should be possible, therefore, to move towards some agreement upon national criteria and a standard assessment instrument.

*Patient characteristics (being very dependent, very old and living alone) predicted an entry to institutional care. This suggests a consensus on the need for institutional care.*

## Delayed discharge

Just over one-quarter of patients (N = 456) were recorded as having their discharge from hospital delayed by three or more days. Team A patients were more likely to have delayed discharges, controlling for patient characteristics. This team may have been slower to set assessment procedures in motion, since this was the team that made the fewest referrals for a care assessment. The analysis showed that two other factors were also independently associated with delayed discharge: not having a family carer and being discharged to institutional care. The absence of a family carer means that a patient cannot be discharged home until he/she is able to manage independently or with help from community services. A family carer also has been identified in the literature on institutional entry as a key decision-maker. The absence of such a person therefore may delay finding a suitable place.

Since entry to institutional care usually involves a major commitment of resources, care managers must send their recommendation up the chain of decision-making. This lack of power by team members over post-hospital resources may contribute to discharge delays. Further, staff from these homes usually visit the hospital to make their own assessment of the patient, which in effect involves a double assessment. The patient also may have to wait until a place becomes available. The delayed discharge associated with entry to a nursing home therefore may have several explanations and warrants further study.

*One quarter of patients were recorded as having their discharge delayed by three or more days. The main factors were the team staffing model, not having a family carer, and being discharged to institutional care. The procedures associated with entry to institutional care are complex and lengthy. These should be further researched to ascertain whether improvements can be made that are in the interests of the patient as well as organisational budgets.*

## Which team model?

Care assessment draws upon staff from different disciplines and so can be undertaken in different ways. Most elderly care teams worked within the *specialist model* usual in a hospital setting where each discipline undertook its own assessment. In a *generalist model* one staff member would undertake all the tasks associated with care assessment. A *multiskill model* was used by a few hospital social services units that employed several types of accredited care assessors: social workers, nurses, and ex-home organisers. The latter units were seeking a greater skill mix in order to bridge the divide between health and social assessment, and in order to divide the workload between 'simple' and 'complex' assessments. Care assessment in hospitals, however, demonstrated little movement to the type of multiskilling approach urged by management consultants.

Care assessment in the case of patients with 'simple' needs (needing only one or two short-term services) was a contested area since several occupational groups claimed competence as a generalist worker: nurse, home care organiser, social worker, and occupational therapist. Staff interviewed from these occupational groups maintained that they had the competence to assess such cases. Further, the argument for a costly multidisciplinary care assessment is less compelling where people need only a single or short-term service. This issue could not be explored in more detail in our patient case review (N = 456), since the great majority of these patients were 'complex' cases: they had multiple needs that required multiple or expensive services. A simplified care assessment model, therefore, may not be appropriate for elderly care units although it may be for some other hospital wards.

Three different multidisciplinary team models were compared where care assessment was coordinated by a different professional. Comparisons have to be made cautiously since many factors come into play such as hospital organisation, the availability of post-hospital health and social care services, and the needs of the patients. The analysis did show, however, that the type of professional influences the services that patients receive.

Team A patients (the nurse-linked team) were least likely, controlling for patient characteristics, to be referred for care assessments, least likely to receive post-hospital health or social care services, and had more discharge delays. The nursing staff themselves spent more time on assessment.

Team B patients (the occupational therapy coordinated team) had the most referrals to occupational therapy and had the most aids and equipment arranged. They were most likely to receive home care irrespective of patient characteristics. But this was also the social services department, with the largest per capita community care budget, and the greater availability of services may have influenced referrals and service outcomes.

Team C patients (social work coordinated) were referred for the most assessments, including a social services assessment, received the greatest range of services, but were not most likely to receive social services. This social services department was experiencing a budget cut, which may have reduced the likelihood of a patient receiving assistance upon discharge.

*Post-hospital social care services for older patients appear to be as much professional-led and services-led as needs-led. On balance, a social work coordinated care assessment process was associated with a more comprehensive multidisciplinary assessment and a greater range, if not amount, of post-hospital assistance.*

'Best practice' guidelines for the care of older people emphasise that decisions should be based upon an assessment of people's 'needs' rather than the predilections of the professional or the available resources. There are several arguments for continuing to regard multidisciplinary assessment as 'best practice'. First, given the tendency for referrals of patients to be professional-led, a multidisciplinary model is important in ensuring that the views of different staff are taken into account when deciding upon post-hospital services. The social work coordinated team undertook care assessments for the largest proportion of patients, more staff were involved in these assessments, and a greater spread of services were received by patients, although this did not result in more patients receiving a greater amount of services. The multi-disciplinary assessment procedure coordinated by the social worker did produce the most 'fine tuning' in matching the needs of vulnerable older patients and post-hospital care services.

# Appendix A.1

**Referral to occupational therapists for assessment by three hospital teams, and referral for assessment to occupational therapists by three hospital teams controlling for patient characteristics**

| | Hospital B v A | | | | Hospital C v A | | | |
|---|---|---|---|---|---|---|---|---|
| | *Odds ratio* | *95% CI* | *Chi-square* | *p* | *Odds ratio* | *95% CI* | *Chi-square* | *p* |
| Crude odds ratio | 8.3 | 3.9–17.6 | 42.4 | 0.00 | 3.9 | 2.0–7.5 | 18.8 | 0.00 |
| *Adjusted odds ratio controlling for patient characteristics* | | | | | | | | |
| *Predisposing factor* | | | | | | | | |
| Age *(85+ years)* *(= yes)* | 8.4 | 3.9–18.1 | 42.6 | 0.00 | 3.9 | 2.0–7.5 | 18.8 | 0.00 |
| *Enabling factors* | | | | | | | | |
| Lives alone *(= yes)* | 7.6 | 3.6–16.2 | 39.0 | 0.00 | 3.7 | 1.9–7.1 | 17.0 | 0.00 |
| No family carer *(= yes)* | 8.1 | 3.8–17.6 | 40.3 | 0.00 | 3.6 | 1.9–7.0 | 16.3 | 0.00 |
| *Health factors* | | | | | | | | |
| 3+ medical conditions *(= yes)* | 9.4 | 4.1–21.6 | 41.8 | 0.00 | 3.8 | 2.0–7.3 | 18.1 | 0.00 |
| Previous admission *(during previous month)* *(= yes)* | 7.7 | 3.7–16.2 | 40.3 | 0.00 | 4.1 | 2.1–8.3 | 19.0 | 0.00 |
| *Functional need on discharge* | | | | | | | | |
| Dependency *(2 or more conditions)* *(= yes)* | 7.7 | 3.6–16.6 | 38.0 | 0.00 | 3.7 | 1.9–7.5 | 16.2 | 0.00 |

# Appendix A.2

**Referral to social services for assessment by three hospital teams, and referral for assessment to social services by three hospital teams controlling for patient characteristics**

| | *Hospital B v A* | | | | *Hospital C v A* | | | |
|---|---|---|---|---|---|---|---|---|
| | *Odds ratio* | *95% CI* | *Chi-square* | *p* | *Odds ratio* | *95% CI* | *Chi-square* | *p* |
| Crude odds ratio | 0.8 | 0.5–1.3 | 0.7 | 0.41 | 5.6 | 2.4–13.3 | 19.5 | 0.00 |
| *Adjusted odds ratio controlling for patient characteristics* | | | | | | | | |
| *Predisposing factor* | | | | | | | | |
| Age *(85+ years)* *(= yes)* | 0.8 | 0.5–1.3 | 0.7 | 0.41 | 5.7 | 2.4–13.5 | 19.5 | 0.00 |
| *Enabling factors* | | | | | | | | |
| Lives alone *(= yes)* | 0.7 | 0.4–1.2 | 1.8 | 0.18 | 5.3 | 2.2–12.8 | 17.8 | 0.00 |
| No family carer *(= yes)* | 0.8 | 0.5–1.3 | 0.9 | 0.34 | 6.4 | 2.5–16.3 | 19.5 | 0.00 |
| *Health factors* | | | | | | | | |
| 3+ medical conditions *(= yes)* | 0.8 | 0.5–1.2 | 1.2 | 0.28 | 5.4 | 2.3–12.9 | 18.5 | 0.00 |
| Previous admission *(during previous month)* *(= yes)* | 0.8 | 0.5–1.3 | 0.7 | 0.40 | 8.0 | 2.8–23.1 | 20.9 | 0.00 |
| *Functional need on discharge* | | | | | | | | |
| Dependency *(2 or more conditions)* *(= yes)* | 0.7 | 0.4–1.2 | 1.9 | 0.17 | 4.4 | 1.9–10.5 | 13.7 | 0.00 |

# Appendix A.3

**Referral for any nursing assessment by three hospital teams, and referral for any nursing assessment by three hospital teams controlling for patient characteristics**

| | *Hospital B v A* | | | | *Hospital C v A* | | | |
|---|---|---|---|---|---|---|---|---|
| | *Odds ratio* | *95% CI* | *Chi-square* | *p* | *Odds ratio* | *95% CI* | *Chi-square* | *p* |
| Crude odds ratio | 2.1 | 1.0–4.4 | 4.3 | 0.04 | 3.8 | 1.8–7.9 | 14.5 | 0.00 |
| *Adjusted odds ratio controlling for patient characteristics* | | | | | | | | |
| *Predisposing factor* | | | | | | | | |
| Age *(85+ years)* *(= yes)* | 2.0 | 1.0–4.2 | 4.0 | 0.05 | 3.8 | 1.8–8.0 | 14.4 | 0.00 |
| *Enabling factors* | | | | | | | | |
| Lives alone *(= yes)* | 2.1 | 1.0–4.3 | 4.1 | 0.04 | 3.8 | 1.8–8.0 | 14.8 | 0.00 |
| No family carer *(= yes)* | 2.1 | 1.0–4.3 | 4.2 | 0.04 | 3.9 | 1.9–8.3 | 15.4 | 0.00 |
| *Health factors* | | | | | | | | |
| 3+ medical conditions *(= yes)* | 2.0 | 1.0–3.9 | 4.5 | 0.04 | 3.6 | 1.8–7.5 | 13.9 | 0.00 |
| Previous admission *(during previous month)* *(= yes)* | 2.0 | 1.0–4.2 | 3.5 | 0.06 | 3.2 | 1.5–7.0 | 9.9 | 0.00 |
| *Functional need on discharge* | | | | | | | | |
| Dependency *(2 or more conditions)* *(= yes)* | 2.2 | 1.1–4.6 | 5.1 | 0.02 | 3.7 | 1.7–7.9 | 12.9 | 0.00 |

# Appendix A.4

**Occupational therapy services arranged by three hospital teams, and occupational therapy services arranged by three hospital teams controlling for patient characteristics**

| | *Hospital B v A* | | | | *Hospital C v A* | | | |
|---|---|---|---|---|---|---|---|---|
| | *Odds ratio* | *95% CI* | *Chi-square* | *p* | *Odds ratio* | *95% CI* | *Chi-square* | *p* |
| Crude odds ratio | 5.6 | 3.3–9.3 | 54.3 | 0.00 | 1.8 | 1.0–3.0 | 4.5 | 0.04 |
| *Adjusted odds ratio controlling for patient characteristics* | | | | | | | | |
| *Predisposing factor* | | | | | | | | |
| Age *(85+ years)* *(= yes)* | 5.6 | 3.3–9.4 | 54.0 | 0.00 | 1.8 | 1.0–3.0 | 4.5 | 0.03 |
| *Enabling factors* | | | | | | | | |
| Lives alone *(= yes)* | 5.5 | 3.3–9.3 | 52.5 | 0.00 | 1.8 | 1.0–3.0 | 4.7 | 0.03 |
| No family carer *(= yes)* | 5.3 | 3.2–8.9 | 49.8 | 0.00 | 1.8 | 1.1–3.1 | 4.9 | 0.03 |
| *Health factors* | | | | | | | | |
| 3+ medical conditions *(= yes)* | 5.7 | 3.3–9.6 | 52.4 | 0.00 | 1.7 | 1.0–2.9 | 4.1 | 0.04 |
| Previous admission *(during previous month)* *(= yes)* | 5.3 | 3.2–8.9 | 50.4 | 0.00 | 1.6 | 0.9–2.7 | 2.8 | 0.10 |
| *Functional need on discharge* | | | | | | | | |
| Dependency *(2 or more conditions)* *(= yes)* | 5.5 | 3.3–9.2 | 52.7 | 0.00 | 1.7 | 1.0–2.9 | 4.2 | 0.04 |

# Appendix A.5

**District nursing services received by patients discharged by three hospital teams, and district nursing services received by patients discharged by three hospital teams controlling for patient characteristics**

| | *Hospital B v A* | | | | *Hospital C v A* | | | |
|---|---|---|---|---|---|---|---|---|
| | *Odds ratio* | *95% CI* | *Chi-square* | *p* | *Odds ratio* | *95% CI* | *Chi-square* | *p* |
| Crude odds ratio | 1.2 | 0.7–1.8 | 0.4 | 0.51 | 1.6 | 0.9–2.6 | 3.0 | 0.08 |
| *Adjusted odds ratio controlling for patient characteristics* | | | | | | | | |
| *Predisposing factor* | | | | | | | | |
| Age *(85+ years)* *(= yes)* | 1.2 | 0.7–1.8 | 0.4 | 0.55 | 1.5 | 0.9–2.5 | 3.0 | 0.08 |
| *Enabling factors* | | | | | | | | |
| Lives alone *(= yes)* | 1.2 | 0.7–1.8 | 0.4 | 0.54 | 1.5 | 0.9–2.4 | 2.3 | 0.13 |
| No family carer *(= yes)* | 1.1 | 0.7–1.8 | 0.2 | 0.62 | 1.5 | 0.9–2.4 | 2.2 | 0.14 |
| *Health factors* | | | | | | | | |
| 3+ medical conditions *(= yes)* | 1.2 | 0.7–1.8 | 0.4 | 0.55 | 1.5 | 0.9–2.5 | 2.6 | 0.11 |
| Previous admission *(during previous month)* *(= yes)* | 1.1 | 0.7–1.8 | 0.2 | 0.64 | 1.5 | 0.9–2.5 | 2.5 | 0.12 |
| *Functional need on discharge* | | | | | | | | |
| Dependency *(2 or more conditions)* *(= yes)* | 1.2 | 0.8–2.0 | 0.9 | 0.36 | 1.8 | 1.1–3.0 | 4..9 | 0.03 |

# Appendix A.6

**Social services received by patients discharged by three hospital teams, and social services received by patients discharged by three hospital teams controlling for patient characteristics**

| | *Hospital B v A* | | | | *Hospital C v A* | | | |
|---|---|---|---|---|---|---|---|---|
| | *Odds ratio* | *95% CI* | *Chi-square* | *p* | *Odds ratio* | *95% CI* | *Chi-square* | *p* |
| Crude odds ratio | 3.1 | 1.9–5.0 | 22.4 | 0.00 | 1.8 | 1.1–3.1 | 4.9 | 0.03 |
| *Adjusted odds ratio controlling for patient characteristics* | | | | | | | | |
| *Predisposing factor* | | | | | | | | |
| Age *(85+ years)* *(= yes)* | 3.1 | 1.9–5.0 | 22.2 | 0.00 | 1.8 | 1.1–3.1 | 4.9 | 0.03 |
| *Enabling factors* | | | | | | | | |
| Lives alone *(= yes)* | 3.0 | 1.8–4.9 | 20.3 | 0.00 | 1.8 | 1.1–3.2 | 5.0 | 0.03 |
| No family carer *(= yes)* | 3.1 | 1.9–5.1 | 21.7 | 0.00 | 1.9 | 1.1–3.2 | 5.3 | 0.02 |
| *Health factors* | | | | | | | | |
| 3+ medical conditions *(= yes)* | 3.2 | 1.9–5.4 | 22.6 | 0.00 | 1.8 | 1.0–3.0 | 4.6 | 0.03 |
| Previous admission *(during previous month)* *(= yes)* | 3.0 | 1.8–4.9 | 21.5 | 0.00 | 1.8 | 1.0–3.0 | 4.2 | 0.04 |
| *Functional need on discharge* | | | | | | | | |
| Dependency *(2 or more conditions)* *(= yes)* | 3.0 | 1.8–4.9 | 20.5 | 0.00 | 1.8 | 1.0–3.1 | 4.6 | 0.03 |

# Appendix A.7

**Institutional care received by patients discharged by three hospital teams, and institutional care received by patients discharged by three hospital teams controlling for patient characteristics**

| | *Hospital B v A* | | | | *Hospital C v A* | | | |
|---|---|---|---|---|---|---|---|---|
| | *Odds ratio* | *95% CI* | *Chi-square* | *p* | *Odds ratio* | *95% CI* | *Chi-square* | *p* |
| Crude odds ratio | 0.9 | 0.5–1.6 | 0.1 | 0.72 | 2.1 | 1.2–3.7 | 7.9 | 0.01 |
| *Adjusted odds ratio controlling for patient characteristics* | | | | | | | | |
| *Predisposing factor* | | | | | | | | |
| Age *(85+ years = yes)* | 0.9 | 0.5–1.6 | 0.1 | 0.80 | 2.2 | 1.3–3.8 | 8.1 | 0.00 |
| *Predisposing Enabling factors* | | | | | | | | |
| Lives alone *(= yes)* | 0.9 | 0.5–1.5 | 0.3 | 0.61 | 2.1 | 1.2–3.8 | 7.5 | 0.01 |
| No family carer *(= yes)* | 0.9 | 0.5–1.6 | 0.1 | 0.79 | 2.2 | 1.2–3.8 | 7.8 | 0.01 |
| *Predisposing Health factors* | | | | | | | | |
| 3+ medical conditions *(= yes)* | 0.9 | 0.5–1.6 | 0.2 | 0.69 | 2.2 | 1.3–3.7 | 8.1 | 0.00 |
| Previous admission *(during previous month) (= yes)* | 0.9 | 0.5–1.5 | 0.2 | 0.67 | 2.0 | 1.1–3.4 | 5.8 | 0.02 |
| *Predisposing Functional need on discharge* | | | | | | | | |
| Dependency *(2 or more conditions) (= yes)* | 0.7 | 0.4–1.3 | 1.5 | 0.22 | 1.5 | 0.8–2.8 | 2.0 | 0.15 |

# Appendix A.8

**Patient discharge delayed by 3 days or more by three hospital teams, and patient discharge delayed by 3 days or more by three hospital teams controlling for patient characteristics**

| | *Hospital B v A* | | | | *Hospital C v A* | | | |
|---|---|---|---|---|---|---|---|---|
| | *Odds ratio* | *95% CI* | *Chi-square* | *p* | *Odds ratio* | *95% CI* | *Chi-square* | *p* |
| Crude odds ratio | 0.2 | 0.1–0.4 | 35.1 | 0.00 | 0.3 | 0.2–0.5 | 19.6 | 0.00 |
| *Adjusted odds ratio controlling for patient characteristics* | | | | | | | | |
| *Predisposing factor* | | | | | | | | |
| Age *(85+ years = yes)* | 0.2 | 0.1–0.4 | 34.3 | 0.00 | 0.3 | 0.2–0.5 | 19.5 | 0.00 |
| *Enabling factors* | | | | | | | | |
| Lives alone *(= yes)* | 0.2 | 0.1–0.4 | 37.9 | 0.20 | 0.3 | 0.2–0.5 | 20.1 | 0.00 |
| No family carer *(= yes)* | 0.2 | 0.1–0.4 | 33.2 | 0.22 | 0.3 | 0.2–0.5 | 17.9 | 0.00 |
| *Health factors* | | | | | | | | |
| 3+ medical conditions *(= yes)* | 0.2 | 0.1–0.4 | 33.8 | 0.00 | 0.3 | 0.2–0.5 | 19.9 | 0.00 |
| Previous admission *(during previous month) (= yes)* | 1.1 | 0.7–1.8 | 0.22 | 0.64 | 1.5 | 0.9–2.5 | 2.5 | 0.12 |
| *Functional need on discharge* | | | | | | | | |
| Dependency *(2 or more conditions) (= yes)* | 0.2 | 0.1–0.4 | 36.7 | 0.00 | 0.3 | 0.1–0.5 | 22.4 | 0.00 |

# References

Abbott, A (1988) *The System of Professions. An Essay on the Division of Expert Labour* University of Chicago Press, Chicago and London.

Alaszewski, A (1995) 'Restructuring health and welfare professions in the United Kingdom' in T Johnson, G Larkins & M Saks (eds) *Health Professions and the State in Europe* Routledge, London & New York.

Alemayehu, E, Molloy, D W, Guyatt, G H, Singer, J, Pennington, G, Basile, J, Eisenmann, M, Finucane, P, McMurdo, M E T, Powell, C, Zelmanowicz, A, Puxty, J, Power, C, Vitou, L, Levenson, S A, Turpie, I D (1991) 'Variability in physicians' decisions on caring for chronically ill elderly patients: an international study' *Canadian Medical Association Journal* 144 (9): 1133–1138.

Alexander, L, Jones, D & Magennis, M (1992) 'The care team' in V Minichiello, L Alexander & D Jones *Gerontology: A Multidisciplinary Approach* Prentice-Hall, Englewood Cliffs, New Jersey.

Allen, I, Hogg, D & Peace, S (1992) *Elderly People: Choice, Participation and Satisfaction* Policy Studies Institute, London.

Armstrong, M (1991) *A Handbook of Personnel Management* Kogan Page, London.

Alter, C F (1990) 'An exploratory study of conflict and coordination in interorganizational service delivery systems' *Academy of Management Journal* 33(3): 478–502.

Arber, S, Gilbert, N & Evandrou, M (1987) 'Gender, household composition, and receipt of domiciliary services by elderly disabled people' *Journal of Social Policy* 17 (2): 153 –175.

Audit Commission (1992a) *Community Care: Managing a Cascade of Change* HMSO, London.

Audit Commission (1992b) *Lying in Wait. The Use of Medical Beds in Acute Hospitals* HMSO, London.

Audit Commission (1996) *Balancing the Care Equation: Progress with Community Care* Community Care Bulletin 3, HMSO, London.

Audit Commission (1997) *The Coming of Age: Improving Services for Older People* Audit Commission, London.

Australian Institute of Health and Welfare (1997) *Aged and Respite Care in Australia: Extracts from Recent Publications* AIHW, Canberra.

Balloch, S, Fisher, M & McLean, J (1999) *The Social Services Working under Pressure* The Policy Press, Bristol.

Bennett, F (1996) *Highly Charged: Policy Issues Surrounding Charging for Non-residential Care* Joseph Rowntree Foundation, York.

Bradshaw, J (1972) 'The concept of social need' *New Society* 30 (March): 640–643.

Brocklehurst, J C, Tallis, R C & Fillit, H M (eds) (1992) *Textbook of Geriatric Medicine and Gerontology* 4th edn, Churchill Livingstone, Edinburgh.

Caldock, K (1996) 'Multidisciplinary assessment and care management, in J Phillips & B Penhale *Reviewing Care Management for Older People* Jessica Kingsley Publishers, London and Bristol.

Carpenter, I & Calnan, M (1997) 'Grey matters' *Health Services Journal* 9 January: 22–23.

Centre for Health Services Research (1996) *Pathways Through Care Study: The Processes and Outcomes of Hospital Care for Older People – An Overview* University of Newcastle upon Tyne.

Chartered Institute of Public Finance and Accounting (1997) *Personal Social Services Statistics* CIPFA, London.

Clark, H, Dyer, S & Hartman, L (1996) *Going Home: Older People Leaving Hospital* Policy Press, University of Bristol in association with the Joseph Rowntree Foundation.

Clements, S (ed) (1977) *Municipal Year Book* 1997 Vol 1, Newman Books, London.

Closs, S J (1997) 'Discharge communications between hospital and community health care staff: a selective review' *Health & Social Care in the Community* 5 (3): 181–197.

Coid, J & Crome, P (1986) 'Bed blocking in Bromley', *British Medical Journal*, 292: 1253–6.

Dalley, G (1991) 'Beliefs and behaviour: professionals and the policy process' *Journal of Ageing Studies* 5 (2): 163–180.

Davies, M (1995) 'The social worker's role in the hospital: seen through the eyes of other healthcare professionals' *Health and Social Care in the Community* 3 (5): 301–309.

Department of Environment (1994) *Index of Local Conditions: An Analysis based on 1991 Census Data* Department of Environment, London.

Department of Health (1989a) *Caring for People: Community Care in the Next Decade and Beyond* White Paper Cmn 849, HMSO, London.

Department of Health (1989b) *Discharge of Patients from Hospital* HC(89)5, LAC(89)7 Department of Health, London.

Department of Health (1992) *The Health of Elderly People: An Epidemiological Overview* HMSO, London.

Department of Health, Local Authority Social Services Letter (1992) *Precondition on the 1993/94 Community Care Special Transitional Grant* (LASSL (92) 11).

Department of Health, Local Authority Social Services Letter (1994) *Precondition on the 1995/96 Community Care Special Transitional Grant* (LASSL (94) 10).

Department of Health (1993) *Caring for People: Information Pack for the Voluntary and Private Sectors* Department of Health, London.

Department of Health (1994) *Hospital Discharge Workbook* Department of Health, London.

Department of Health (1995a) *Statistical Bulletin: NHS Hospital Activity Statistics* Department of Health, London.

Department of Health (1995b) *NHS Responsibilities for Meeting Continuing Health Care Needs* HSG(95)8, LAC(95)5 Department of Health, London.

Department of Health (1996a) *Statistical Bulletin: Community Care Statistics* Department of Health, London.

Department of Health (1996b) *NHS Responsibilities for Meeting Continuing Health Care Needs: Current Progress and Future Priorities* EL (96)8, Cl (96)5 Department of Health, London.

Department of Health (1996c) *Health and Personal Social Services Statistics for England 1996 edition* The Stationery Office, London.

Department of Health (1996d) *Hospital Episode Statistics: Volume 2*, Department of Health, London.

Department of Health (1997a) *Better Value for Money in Social Services: A Review of Performance Trends in Social Services in England* Department of Health, London.

Department of Health (1997b) *The New NHS: Modern, Dependable* Cm 3807 The Stationery Office, London.

Department of Health, Personal Social Services Local Authority Statistics (1997c) *Community Care Statistics: Day and Domiciliary Personal Social Services for Adults* Government Statistical Service, London.

Department of Health Executive Letter (1997d) *Better Services for Vulnerable People* (EL(97)62).

Department of Health (1998) *Health and Personal Social Services Statistics for England* 1998 edn. The Stationery Office, London.

Department of Trade and Industry, Consumer Safety Unit (1997) *19th Annual Report: Home Accident Surveillance System 1995* DTI, London.

Futter, C & Penhale, B (1996) 'Needs-led assessment: the practitioner's perspective' in J Phillips & B Penhale (eds) *Reviewing Management for Older People* Jessica Kingsley Publishers, London and Bristol.

Hall, R H (1986) 'Interorganizational or interprofessional relationships: a case of mistaken identity? In W R Scott & B L Black (eds) *The Organization of Mental Health Services: Societal and Community Systems*, Sage, Beverly Hills.

Harding, T (1997) *A Life Worth Living: The Independence and Inclusion of Older People* Help the Aged, London.

Harrison, A & Prentice, S (1998) *Hospital Policy in the United Kingdom: Its Development, Its Future* Transaction Publishers, New Brunswick and London.

Headrick, L A, Wilcock, P M & Batalden, P B (1988) 'Interprofessional working and continuing medical education' *British Medical Journal* V316: 771–774.

Healy, J (1994) 'Who gets what? Comparing aged care community service fields in Adelaide and Melbourne' *Lincoln Papers in Gerontology* No. 25, Lincoln Gerontology Centre, La Trobe University, Melbourne.

Henwood, M & Wistow, G (1993) *Hospital Discharge and Community Care: Early Days* Nuffield Institute for Health, and Social Services Inspectorate.

Henwood, M (1994) *Fit For Change? Snapshots of the Community Care Reforms One Year On* Kings Fund/Nuffield Institute for Health.

Henwood, M (1995) *Making a Difference? Implementation of the Community Care Reforms Two Years On* Kings Fund/Nuffield Institute for Health, London.

Henwood, M (1996) *Continuing Health Care: Analysis of a sample of official documents* Department of Health, London.

Hokenstad, M C & Ritvo, R (eds) (1982) *Linking Health Care and Social Services: International Perspectives* Sage, Beverly Hills.

House of Commons Health Committee (1996) *Long-term Care: Future Provisions and Funding* Third Report, HMSO, London.

Institute of Health Services Management (1996) *The IHSM Health Services Yearbook 1995/1996* IHSM, London.

Impallomeni, M & Starr, J (1995) 'The changing face of community and institutional care for the elderly' *Journal of Public Health Medicine* 17 (2): 171–178.

Jones, D A et al (1993) 'Patients' opinion of hospital care and discharge' *European Journal of Gerontology* 2(l): 24.

Joseph Rowntree Foundation Inquiry (1996) *Meeting the Costs of Continuing Care* JRF, York.

Kane, R A (1985) 'Assessing the elderly client' in A Monk (ed) *Handbook of Gerontological Research* Van Nostrand Reinhold, New York.

Kane, R A (1995) 'Expanding the home care concept: blurring distinctions among home care, institutional care, and other long-term care services' *The Millbank Quarterly* 23(2): 161–186.

Kid, C B (1962) 'Misplacement of elderly in hospitals', *British Medical Journal*, 2: 1491–2.

Laing & Buisson (1996) *Care of Elderly People Market Survey 1996* Laing & Buisson, London.

Laing & Buisson (1997) *Care of Elderly People Market Survey 1997* Laing & Buisson, London.

Lever, J A, Molloy, D W, Eisenmann, McMurdo, M E T, Finucane, P, Guyatt G H, Rees, L & Horsman, J R (1992) 'Variability in nurses' decisions about the care of chronically ill elderly patients: an international study' *Humane Science* 8 (2): 138–144.

Lewis, J, Bernstock, P, Bovell, V & Wookey, F (1996) 'The purchaser/provider split in social care: is it working?' *Social Policy and Administration* 30(1): 1–53.

Lonsdale, S, Webb, A & Briggs, T L (eds) (1980) *Teamwork in the Personal Services and Health Care: British and American Perspectives* Croom Helm, London.

Means R & Smith R (1998a) *From Poor Law to Community Care* 2nd edition, Policy Press, Bristol.

Means R & Smith R (1998b) *Community Care: Policy and Practice* 2nd edition, Macmillan, Basingstoke.

Moxley, D P (1989) *The Practice of Case Management* Sage, Beverly Hills.

Murphy E (1977) 'Blocked beds' *British Medical Journal*, 292, 1395–1396.

National Association of Health Authorities and Trusts (1995) *Health Authorities' Perspectives on Community Care* NAHAT, UK.

Neill, J & Williams, J (1992) *Leaving Hospital: Elderly People and their Discharge to Community Care* HMSO, London.

Netten, A & Dennett, J (1996) *Unit Costs of Health and Social Care* Personal Social Services Research Unit, University of Kent, Canterbury.

Netten, A & Dennett, J (1997) *Unit Costs of Health and Social Care* Personal Social Services Research Unit, University of Kent, Canterbury.

NHS Health Advisory Service (1997) *Addressing the Balance: the multidisciplinary assessment of elderly people and the delivery of high quality continuing care* HMSO, London.

Nolan, M & Caldock, K (1996) 'Assessment: identifying the barriers to good practice' *Health and Social Care in the Community* 4 (2): 77–85.

Office for National Statistics (1998) *Social Trends 28* The Stationery Office, London.

Organisation for Economic Co-operation and Development (1993) *OECD Health Systems: Facts and Trends* OECD, Paris.

OPCS (1996) *Living in Britain: Results from the 1994 General Household Survey* HMSO, London.

Øvretveit, J (1993) *Coordinating Community Care: Multidisciplinary Teams and Care Management* Open University Press, Buckingham.

Øvretveit, J (1997) 'How to describe interprofessional working' in Øvretveit J, Mathias, P & Thompson, T (eds) *Interprofessional Working for Health and Social Care* Macmillan, Basingstoke.

Perrow, C (1986) *Complex Organizations: A Critical Essay* 3rd edn, Random House, New York.

Petch, A (1996) 'New concepts, old responses: assessment and care management pilot projects in Scotland' in J Phillips & B Penhale *Reviewing Care Management for Older People* Jessica Kingsley Publishers, London and Bristol.

Poulton, B C & West, M A (1993a) 'Effective multidisciplinary teamwork in primary health care' *Journal of Advanced Nursing* 18: 918–925.

Poulton, B C & West M A (1993b) 'Primary health care team effectiveness: developing a constituency approach' *Health and Social Care* 2: 77–84.

Qualls, S H & Czirr, R (1988) 'Geriatric health teams: classifying models of professional and team functioning' *The Gerontologist* 28 (3): 373–379.

Rachman, R (1995) 'Community care: changing the role of hospital social work' *Health & Social Care in the Community* 3: 163–172.

Royal College of Physicians & British Geriatrics Society (1992) *Standardised Assessment Scales for Elderly People* Royal College of Physicians & British Geriatrics Society, London.

Royal Commission on Long Term Care, Sutherland Report (1999) *With Respect to Old Age: Long Term Care: Rights and Responsibilities* The Stationery Office, London.

Skinner, K M, Tennstedt, S L & Crawford, S L (1994) 'Do characteristics of informal caregivers affect the length of hospital stay for frail elders?' *Journal of Ageing and Health* 6 (2): 255–269.

Social Services Inspectorate, (1991) *Care Management and Assessment: Managers' Guide; Practitioners' Guide; Summary of Practice Guidance* Department of Health, London.

Social Services Inspectorate (1993) *Monitoring and Development: Special Study of 31 December Agreements, Reviewing the Implementation* Department of Health, London.

Social Services Inspectorate/Department of Health (1995) *Moving On: Report of the National Inspection of Social Services Department Arrangements for the Discharge of Older People from Hospital to Residential or Nursing Home Care*, Department of Health, London.

*Social Services Yearbook 1997* Pitman Publishing, London.

Stallknecht, K (1992) 'Nursing in Europe' in T Richards (ed) *Medicine in Europe* British Medical Journal, London.

Steering Group Report (1996) *The Future Healthcare Workforce* Health Services Management Unit University of Manchester.

Taraborrelli P et al (1999) *Hospital Discharge for Frail Older People*, The Stationery Office, London.

Tennstedt, S L, Sullivan, L M, McKinlay, J B & D'Agostino, R B (1990) 'How important is functional status as a predictor of service use by older people?' *Journal of Ageing and Health* 2(4):439–461.

Tester, S (1996) *Community Care for Older People* Macmillan, Basingstoke.

Townsend, J, Piper, M, Frank, A O, Dyer, S, North W R S, Meade, T W (1988) 'Reduction in hospital readmission stay of elderly patients by a community-based hospital discharge scheme randomised controlled trial' *British Medical Journal* 297: 545–547.

Thomas M, Walker A, Wilmot A, Bennet N (1998) *Living in Britain: Results from the 1996 General Household Survey* Stationery Office, London.

Twigg, J & Atkin, K (1994) *Carers Perceived: Policy and Practice in Informal Care* Open University Press, Buckingham, UK.

Walston S & Kimberley J (1997) 'Re-engineering hospitals: experience and analysis from the field' *Hospital and Health Service Administration* 42: 143–163.

Victor, C R (1994) *Old Age in Modern Society: A Textbook of Social Gerontology* 2nd edn, Chapman & Hall, London.

Victor, C R (1997) *Community Care and Older People* S Thorne, Cheltenham.

Zucker, L G eds (1988) *Institutional Patterns and Organizations: Culture and Environment* Ballinger, Cambridge, Massachusetts.